T0247473

Late Beauty

Selected Poems of
Tuvia Ruebner

Translated from the Hebrew by
Lisa Katz and Shahar Bram

Zephyr Press | Brookline, Mass.

Cover photograph Copyright © by Tuvia Ruebner
Book design by *type*slowly
Printed in Michigan by Cushing Malloy, Inc.

Earlier versions of some of the translations have appeared in *The Drunken Boat, Mississippi Review Online* (now called *New World Writing*), *Poetry International Rotterdam* and in the book, *The Ambassadors of Death*, by Shahar Bram (Sussex Academic Press, 2011).

Zephyr Press acknowledges with gratitude the financial support of The National Endowment for the Arts, the Massachusetts Cultural Council, and the Little Strettin Fund.

Zephyr Press, a non-profit arts and education 501(c)(3) organization, publishes literary titles that foster a deeper understanding of cultures and languages. Zephyr books are distributed to the trade in the U.S. and Canada by Consortium Book Sales and Distribution [www.cbsd.com].

Cataloguing-in publication data is available from the Library of Congress.

ZEPHYR PRESS
www.zephyrpress.org

CONTENTS

Introduction

Lisa Katz and Shahar Bram

Ideas emanate from Tuvia Ruebner's lyric poems in lines that are lucid but also mask personal secrets. Ruebner's poetry blooms and overflows out of its subjects and interrogates the way history intertwines with the accidental, circumstantial nature of any one life and the making of art, from European masterpieces to tourist postcards. No matter what he looks at—including a soccer game between teams from Uruguay and Ghana, or the Israeli-Palestinian conflict as it plays out in Hebron—he connects his particular ghosts to philosophic questions.

"The dead are not mute if we are not deaf," writes Ruebner in his autobiography, *A Long Short Life.*[1] The Israeli poet survived the Holocaust as a teenager by immigrating to Palestine. His extended family was murdered, and so he has had many voices to listen to, even taking into account his advanced age (ninety-three as this book goes to print). It is understandable that an awareness of loss and death might permeate his work, but the poems in this selection reflect, at the same time, his photographer's eye and unique appreciation of art.

Ruebner was born in multi-ethnic Bratislava, Slovakia, in 1924, with German as his mother tongue, a language in which he began to write, mostly prose, as a child. (When the poet was ten years old, a teacher sent a short story of his to a well-known newspaper, but the editor rejected it, not believing that a child could have written so well.) Ruebner terms his family's Jewish household "semi-secular." His mother's parents were observant Jews; his father was a member of the local Freemason Lodge. In April 1941, along with eight other young Jews with legal entrance certificates into British Mandate Palestine awaiting them in Budapest, he was able to leave Slovakia. The country, then part of the Axis with Nazi Germany, was not yet committed to the deportation of its nearly 90,000

---

1. *Ein langes kurzes Leben*, Aachen, Rimbaud, 2004. *Haim arukim k'tsarim* [in Hebrew] Tel Aviv, Keshev Publishing House, 2006.

Jews to concentration camps, and occasionally awarded payment to the German regime for the release of Jews. (The Germans sometimes actually released them. Mass deportations to the east would occur in 1942). After a journey that took the young people through Romania, Turkey, Syria and Lebanon, they arrived in Palestine. Ruebner was sent to Kibbutz Merhavia in the northern part of the country, which became his permanent home.

Ruebner continued to write in German until about a dozen years after his arrival, when he began to write original poetry in Hebrew. To this day, he translates his work into German, and all of it has been published in Germany. In Hebrew, he is the author of fifteen volumes of poetry, two photograph albums, and a monograph on the poetry of his close friend, writer-scholar Lea Goldberg, as well as other literary criticism and translations (of S.J. Agnon from Hebrew into German, and of Goethe, Ludwig Strauss and Friedrich Schlegel from German into Hebrew). The poet has also written an autobiography in which he speaks directly about the presence of death in his life. Emeritus Professor of Hebrew and Comparative Literature at Haifa University and an accomplished photographer since his teenage years, Ruebner has been awarded his country's highest honor, the Israel Prize in 2008, as well as numerous literary awards, and has received international recognition as well, including the Konrad Adenauer Literature Prize in 2012, bestowed by the German government.

Ruebner's parents, grandparents and sister—his immediate family—were murdered by the Nazis in the Holocaust, and he later lost close family members to what are usually considered individual, unhistorical tragedies: his first wife was killed in a fiery bus accident early in their marriage, when their daughter was an infant, and one of his sons from his second marriage disappeared in Ecuador while travelling more than thirty years ago. Most of the friends Ruebner made after arriving in Palestine have predeceased him, including two great Hebrew poet-scholars who were very close to him personally and professionally: Lea Goldberg and Dan Pagis.

Ruebner's special talent lies in his ability to seriously question moral pieties. In his postcard series, for example, "Postcard from the Hebron Area" opens with the neutral line: "Hebron is a very ancient city." The second line provides the city's biblical pedigree as the burial place of Abraham and Sarah, apparently accepted by the speaker: "Our father Abraham is buried there with his wife Sarah." But the sentence does not end at the end of the line. It is enjambed, and its continuation identifies the assertion as a mere claim, made by others: "they say." In this way, the speaker, who identifies with the biblical figures of "our" Abraham and Sarah, at the same time distances himself from those who make biblical claims to territory, and emphasizes the story's mythical nature. Immediately following, the poet points out the irony of the sacred nature of a site that is also a material marker of mortality, and the deadly political/religious conflict that has ensued in the wake of its presumed spirituality: "Very holy for a land that lives off death." The Hebron poem is a protest verse, which Ruebner has often written and continues to produce as this book goes to press.

As to the larger picture, Ruebner has suggested a way to locate his work in the canon of twentieth-century Hebrew poetry, and what sets it apart from other Israeli poetry.

He defines himself as heir to a particular European tradition that concentrates on emotion at the expense of explicit narrative and a narrow focus on the self. In a 2014 radio interview with Anat Sharon-Blais,[2] Ruebner points to German expressionism, which he studied at Hebrew University under German Jewish refugees Werner Kraft and Ludwig Strauss, as a characteristic of his work that separates it from Israeli-Anglo-American poetics. During the radio talk, Ruebner termed the dominant trends in Israeli poetry "narcissistic."

In a *Tablet* interview with Toby Perl Freilich that same year,[3] Ruebner further defined his German literary background as a marker of the difference between his work and that of other Israeli poets of his generation such as Yehuda Amichai and Natan Zach, who also arrived in the country as native speakers of German. "I come from a German tradition," Ruebner told Perl Freilich. "They, though native German speakers, were formed more by an Anglo-Saxon/British one. We read different poets. [The influential Hebrew poet Natan] Alterman . . . had] rich imaginative powers, but no

---

2. Tuvia Ruebner, 90th birthday interview with Anat Sharon-Blais on iCast, January 4, 2014: http://www.icast.co.il/default.aspx?p=Podcast&id=319148&cid=462844

3. "Tuvia Ruebner Never Stops Mourning the Lost," by Toby Perl Freilich, *Tablet Magazine*, May 12, 2014: http://tabletmag.com/jewish-arts-and-culture/books/172169/tuvia-ruebner-never-stops-mourning-the-lost

soul, no *Innigkeit*, [interior depth]. I like [Lea] Goldberg because she's closer to the Russian/German tradition of *Innigkeit*—like the pianissimo of Mahler." The day after his conversation with the journalist, the poet wrote her to add that "I saw everything through the prism of Auschwitz, and they didn't."

Ruebner also belongs to a broader, international group of multilingual writers. Mass migrations, whether for political, economic or other reasons, have led to varying degrees of multilingualism everywhere. In Israel, this is expressed by numerous Hebrew writers who heard one or more other languages at home, and may read other languages as well. Most modern poets writing in Hebrew who were born at any time from the end of the 19th century through the middle of the 20th century (or even later) were born into a multilingual situation, whether abroad, in Mandate Palestine or the state of Israel.

Ruebner writes free verse in modern Hebrew; he began to translate it into German, he often tells visitors, after others had begun to do so and he realized it emerged as poetry in his first language as well. Some of the issues involved in translating his work into English are matters of culture-based information and not linguistic. Ruebner is well aware of this. In the original Hebrew poem, "Postcard from Vienna," there is a line saying: "A *victim* doesn't have to be ashamed because he was/ a *victim*" (emphasis ours). In the English translation, however, the poet asked us to replace the word "victim" with the word "hangman." Ruebner believes that his ironic reference to the Austrian collaborators with the Nazis, who after the war saw themselves as victims, would be lost on contemporary readers.

It may seem an odd thing to say about poetry, but the strengths of Ruebner's works are not dependent on language. It is for linguists to examine whether or not this stems from the fact that his mother tongue is German, a cousin of English (as was the case for Yehuda Amichai, Hebrew's most translated and popular poet, and Dan Pagis, less familiar if more complex). Most of his poems use a conversational register. The poems are philosophical, and concepts may be conveyed in any language. Some offer beauty and wisdom on an aesthetically pleasing surface, and then question ideas of beauty, wisdom and aesthetics. Some poems are mysterious, some jarring. And some are intellectual puzzles. Most are all of the above.

This book began in the summer of 2006, when we—Lisa Katz, an American-Israeli literary translator and Shahar Bram, a Haifa University lecturer, both poets—began collaborating on the translation of a dozen ekphrastic poems by Tuvia Ruebner. Bram invited Katz to work on the translations for a monograph he was writing.[4] Katz, who had previously translated a love poem by Ruebner ("I didn't expect," included in this volume), agreed, making English drafts that we discussed extensively and reworked together. Bram picked most of the poems to be translated, in conjunction with his scholarly work on Ruebner's interest in particular modes: ekphrasis and the postcard form. We also picked poems with reference to Ruebner's family history and the Holocaust, and poems we liked because of their universal lyricism. The resulting manuscript was submitted to Ruebner for his approval. Finally, co-publisher Leora Zeitlin reviewed the manuscript and made suggestions.

While many collections are organized chronologically, this book is not. "Chronology is dead. I have never organized my books by chronology, rather the associations among the poems," Ruebner has said. His memoir is also not chronological, because, he explains in that book, "Memory doesn't acknowledge chronological time. It jumps forward and backwards as it wishes." Accordingly, this book begins with poems from the last decade that raise questions about time and poetry, respectively, and continues with poems grouped roughly into three areas of Ruebner's literary focus, rather than chronological order: a selection of his postcard poems, another section dominated by his ekphrastic work, and poems that deal more directly with his personal history, memory and loss. The poems in this collection span the last 45 years of Ruebner's writing, and are culled from seven of his books. The title of our book, *Late Beauty*, is a version of the title of a relatively recent volume, *Yofi Meukhar*, which may also be translated "belated beauty." Interestingly, the one poem we translated from that book, "On Time," first appeared in Ruebner's 2005 *Selected Poems* and was rewritten by him and published in its slightly altered form a few years later. We translated the newer version.

---

4. Shahar Bram, *The Ambassadors of Death: The Sister Arts, Western Canon, and the Silent Lines of a Hebrew Survivor*, Trans. Batya Stein, Brighton: Sussex Academic Press, 2011. The Hebrew version was published in Israel by Keshev Press in 2014.

The title of the Ruebner volume *Statue and Mask* (*Pesel u-Masekha*, 1983), from which many of the ekphrastic poems in this book are taken, refers to and rebels against the divine call: "Thou shalt not make unto thee any graven image, or any likeness of any thing . . ." (Exodus 20:4-5). A Jewish poet, Bram noted in his monograph, has dedicated an entire book of poems to pictures and statues, which is, in a sense, a challenge to God. Ruebner, he suggests, "addresses the Jewish experience in a century when God hid his face," and "turns his personal trauma into a broad world view that settles accounts with Western culture." Furthermore, "the ekphrastic description [takes] the place of the confessing lyrical subject,"[5] which as Ruebner has explicitly stated, is not integral to his own poetics. And Ruebner's photography, a profession he originally studied because he thought it would help him earn a living, enhanced his natural ability to see works of art.

For example, the sight of the marble torsos of Greek statues during a visit to a museum sparks a richly-layered poem, "The Youths." In the first stanza, they are "always smiling." Though they are *of* humans, the statues are inhuman. Ruebner personifies them, attributing smiles and hearts and movement, and describing them as (museum) "entrance guards" albeit "of dreams." This is a natural response to art, particularly when it is mimetic or realistic in form. The dreams, however, provide a twist. They are those of the visitors to the museum; that is, they are ours.

The associative realm of dreams (like the associative nature of poetry) opens the poem to more complex subjects, ones that have somehow escaped the range of responses to beautiful art objects. In this sense the role of the statues as "entrance guards"—figures who would limit us to seeing the benign and prosaic elements of life (smiling, walking, resting) — has failed. Indeed, the second stanza begins with a jarring switch of venue and the introduction of a heavily freighted, specific character, "the son":

> On Sunday morning the son left the country
> [...]
> There's no way to know when he'll return.
> A small smile is hidden inside his face.
> All kinds of legends are spreading.

---

5. *The Ambassadors of Death*, 8-9.

A lost son is a real-life tragedy that Ruebner has experienced. It is also a tragedy of mythic proportions, and its existence in myth hints at meanings larger than any individual life. The final stanza fulfills the expectation raised by "all kinds of legends" and alludes to Aegeus, the father of Theseus. Aegeus, the myth goes, once nearly poisoned his own son, and later committed suicide when he mistakenly thought that Theseus had died (in battle with the Minotaur on Crete). Theseus, however, was not dead, but had simply forgotten to change a black sail for a white one to indicate his victory. Here, an ordinary human failing, a matter of happenstance rather than deep meaning, has created a personal tragedy. Ruebner is certainly writing about helplessness in the face of human evil, but also about simple human failure.

In "The Ambassadors," which was the first poem that we translated, Ruebner considers a Hans Holbein painting of 1553 that hangs in the National Gallery of London. The opening line—"I don't know where to begin"—is that of the poet-speaker, who questions his enterprise in real time: how does a poet begin a poem? With this deceptively simple opening line, Ruebner interests the reader in a common dilemma: where are any of us to begin anything? And his particular dilemma, how shall I start my poem, raises the question of where the beginning of a painting is located. Do we "read" them according to some spatial order, from top to bottom, from left to right or right to left? Perspective, therefore, is one of the subjects investigated by a poem about a painting that itself offers a visual perspective on political power.

This poem describes a painting of two ambassadors—Jean de Dinteville and Georges de Selve—and the many objects, symbolic and otherwise, that are placed around them. But Ruebner's second line heads straight for the deviant element in the painting, which happens to be on the bottom. "The main thing is the skull. But / why this angle?" The short opening stanza focuses on the distorted skull at the bottom of the frame, which looks to us like a flat disk, a CD or DVD, lifting up at a gravity-defying angle from the patterned floor where the two male subjects stand. Its anamorphic perspective requires the viewer to look at the painting from the side in order to see that the object is in fact a skull. Ruebner again focuses on the structures of art that apply to both poem and painting, as well as an important topic: what's your angle, that is, what is your point of view?

Why do you, or we, have this particular vantage and how does this make us perceive the world differently?

The poem ends by noting that the skull is an image of death that chokes the viewer who stands "on the right" (in the "right" place?), though it looks like simply "something unrecognizable,/ some kind of a yellowish spot casting a shadow" to others. The poem ends with the line, "A wordless madness slaughters the picture."

Ruebner's series of postcard poems are of recent vintage, appearing in the volumes, *Late Poems* (1999) and *Contradictory Poems* (2011). They provide him with another framework related to the connection between writing and the visual arts. They also remind us of the 24-word missives that Ruebner was able to send to his family in Europe via the Red Cross. The poet continued to send them for two years after replies ceased, unaware that his parents and sister had been murdered in 1942.

In "Postcard to my Soul Mate," while the speaker may be presumed to be writing to a close friend or lover, he refers in the opening line to "a postcard from Paris" that he or they have received from someone else, a third person. The poem *is* the postcard and also *about* a postcard. And Paris turns out to be not the real Paris, but "Paris des rêves"—the Paris of dreams, the existence of which as a reverie Ruebner emphasizes by offering the words both in French and in translation. Even worse, the speaker's partner in dialogue identifies the picture on the card as London, and not Paris, which leads the speaker to question the reality of his memory entirely.

In other postcard poems, Ruebner recreates scenes from his youth, other European places he has visited, and Palestine/Israel, where he has lived for seventy-six years. Ruebner notes the exaggerated ethereality of Jerusalem, and questions the validity of deadly political claims to the city of Hebron.

The different threads of Tuvia Ruebner's life story emerge in the lyric poems at the end of this selection of his work. "The Shining Day," for example, first published when the poet was in his seventies, features an unspecified "boatman" and evokes a crossing into the underworld. In it, a child "still thinks she can/ get away," causing us to think of his little sister, murdered in the Holocaust. In "Photo" and "Rainy Day and a Photo," too, there is "a boy's face" and "a child's face"—perhaps that of his lost son?

In an interview with the Israeli daily, *Haaretz*, in 2005, Ruebner reflects on the subjects of place and dislocation that reverberate in all his poetry, summing up laconically that "I am here [in Israel] because I am here. Poetry has become my homeland."[6]

In this poetic expanse, Ruebner embeds his particular life story within the enormity of 20th-century, and now, 21st-century, history, of both Europe and contemporary Israel. And like the great works of art he often describes, his works captivate us with their beauty, while also containing images of personal loss and violence. "Why are you drawn toward it,/ dreamstruck?" he asks in the poem "Why," about an attraction to a Mayan artifact, a paradoxically beautiful skull. According to an earlier line in the poem, it "gives shape to silence." This is a fitting description of Ruebner's art as well. By "giving shape to silence," Ruebner's work invites us into a place of remembrance—of lost family and friends and former life, where now, as he wrote in his autobiography, the "dead are not mute." At the same time, he reminds us that "the darkness so dark," reflected in the eye sockets of the Mayan skull and in his poetry, still reigns.

6. "Poetry Became My Homeland," by Dalia Karpel, *Haaretz* English edition, May 19, 2005: http://www.haaretz.com/poetry-became-my-homeland-1.158905

Late Beauty

עַל הַזְּמַן

1

אַתָּה שׁוֹאֵל אוֹתִי עַל הַזְּמַן?
הוּא לֹא חָבֵר שֶׁלִּי. לָמָּה לְדַבֵּר עַל הַזְּמַן?
כִּי אֵין לוֹ פַּרְצוּף? כִּי לְעוֹלָם לֹא יַבִּיט
עַיִן בְּעַיִן וּלְפֶתַע יַכֶּה וּמִיָּד יִטְעַן
כִּי אֵין כָּמוֹהוּ לְרַפֵּא אֶת הַפֶּצַע?
לוֹחֵשׁ עַל אָזְנֶיךָ נֶחָמוֹת קְטַנּוֹת
וּבִמְחִי יָד מוֹעֵךְ אֶת גּוּפְךָ
וּמַשְׁלִיךְ אוֹתְךָ לְאֵיזוֹ זָוִית שְׁכוּחָה?

2

הַבֵּן, הַבֵּן הַשּׁוֹאֵל "מָה פִּתְאֹם?" אַחֲרֵי
חִבּוּק הַפְּרֵדָה אָז בִּנְמַל הַתְּעוּפָה הַזָּר —
זֶה, זֶה הַזְּמַן.
זֶה הַזְּמַן הָעוֹמֵד וְאֵינֶנּוּ זָז.
זֶה הַזְּמַן בְּלִי זְמַן.
אוֹי לְכָל הַחֲכָמִים הַמְנַסִּים לוֹמַר דְּבָרִים
חֲכָמִים אוֹ שְׁנוּנִים.
וַי לְכָל הַחָכְמָה הַזֹּאת.

3

אֵיזֶה חֲלוֹם מָתוֹק לְמִי שֶׁאֵינֶנּוּ מַחֲזִיק מַעֲמָד
בַּמָּקוֹם שֶׁנִּמְצָא בּוֹ, קְצַר רוּחַ, מְבַקֵּשׁ
לָצֵאת מֵעוֹרוֹ וְתוֹקֵעַ עֵינַיִם בִּמְחוֹג הַשְּׁנִיּוֹת
הָרָץ רָץ רָץ כְּמוֹ רוֹדֵף אֶת צִלּוֹ
רַק הָלְאָה, רַק הָלְאָה מִזֶּה
רַק הָלְאָה, תָּמִיד הָלְאָה
תָּמִיד, תָּמִיד
לַמָּקוֹם שֶׁמִּמֶּנּוּ בָּא.

On Time

1.

Are you asking me about time?
It's no friend of mine. Why talk
about faceless time? Because it will never look you in the eye,
but suddenly strikes and claims
there's nothing like it to heal wounds?
Because it whispers sweet consolations in your ear,
crushes your body in one blow,
and tosses it away at a forsaken angle?

2.

The son, the son asking "What's this?"
after a parting embrace. Then, at a foreign airport —
this, this is time.
This is time standing still.
This is timeless time.
Too bad for all the wise people who try to say
smart or clever things.
Woe to all this knowledge.

3.

What a sweet dream for the one who can't last
in his situation, impatient, he seeks
to shed his skin and fix his eyes on the second hand of the clock
which runs on as if chasing its shadow
onward only, away from here,
only onward, always onward
always, always
to the place it came from.

אורוגוואי-גאנה 2010

אֵין כֹּרַח לִכְתֹב שִׁיר עַל כַּדּוּרֶגֶל
גַּם בְּהִתְקַיֵּם הַמּוּנְדִיאָל 2010.
הֲרֵי רֹב רֻבָּם שֶׁל הַצּוֹפִים מִסְתַּדְּרִים
לְלֹא שִׁירִים, בָּרוּךְ הַשֵּׁם.
אֲבָל אִם אֹמַר בְּשִׁירִי לַכַּדּוּרַגְלָן הַשָּׁחֹר מִגָּאנָה
כִּי רָצִיתִי מְאֹד שֶׁקְּבוּצָתוֹ תְּנַצַּח, וְכִי הַשּׁוֹפֵט
יָכוֹל הָיָה לִקְבֹּעַ "שַׁעַר" כְּשֶׁכַּדּוּרוֹ הַנִּפְלָא
נֶחְסַם לֹא בִּידֵי הַשּׁוֹעֵר אֶלָּא בְּתוֹךְ הַשַּׁעַר פְּנִימָה
בִּידָיו שֶׁל שַׂחְקָן אוּרוּגְוָאִי רָגִיל...
לַחֲקִים יֵשׁ פֵּרוּשֵׁי פֵּרוּשִׁים וְאָסוּר שֶׁיִּטְשְׁטֵשׁ הַהֶבְדֵּל
בֵּין חֹק לַעֲרִיצוּת. לָכֵן יָכוֹל הָיָה הַשּׁוֹפֵט לְוַתֵּר
עַל הַכַּרְטִיס הָאָדֹם – הַמִּשְׂחָק הָיָה צִבְעוֹנִי דַּיּוֹ –
וּלְוַתֵּר עַל הַפֶּנָדֶּל עִם הַקּוֹרָה הַקַּנָּאִית.
אוֹ אָז, אָחִי, אִשְׁתְּךָ הָיְתָה מְחַדֵּשׁ אֶת אַהֲבָתָהּ
אַהֲבָה גֵּאָה כְּמוֹ דְּרוֹם-אָמֵרִיקָאִית, וּמְחַבֶּקֶת אוֹתְךָ
גַּם אַחֲרֵי הַמִּשְׂגָּל הַשְּׁבִיעִי בִּפְנֵי בְּתוּלָה מְאִירוֹת
וּבִנְךָ הָיָה נוֹשֵׂא עֵינָיו אֵלֶיךָ כְּאוֹמֵר:
אֵין עוֹד אַבָּא כָּמוֹךָ. וַחֲבֵרֶיךָ הָיוּ מַזְמִינִים לִשְׁתּוֹת
עַל חֶשְׁבּוֹנָם וְשָׁרִים אִתְּךָ עַד אוֹר הַבֹּקֶר
וְלִישֹׁן הָיִיתָ הוֹלֵךְ בְּהַרְגָּשָׁה מְתוּקָה שֶׁחַיֶּיךָ
לֹא לַשָּׁוְא הָיוּ, אַדְּרַבָּא, הֵם יָפִים, הֵם יָפִים יָפִים
וְיָדַיִם פְּסוּלוֹת לֹא תּוּכַלְנָה לִגְרֹעַ כְּקָרֶט מִיָּפְיָם.
כָּל זֶה עָשׂוּי הָיָה לִקְרוֹת לוּ קָרֵאתָ שִׁירָה עִבְרִית
אוֹ לַחֲלוּפִין לוּ כּוֹתֵב הָיִיתִי אֲנִי שִׁיר בִּשְׂפַת אַשַׁנְטִי.

Uruguay-Ghana 2010

There's no need to write a poem about soccer
even during the World Cup.
Most of the spectators manage
without poetry, thank God.
But I'd tell the player from Ghana
that I really wanted his team to win, and that the referee
should have awarded him a goal when his fabulous kick
was blocked not by the goalkeeper but inside
at the hands of an ordinary Uruguayan player . . .
There are many ways to interpret rules and one mustn't blur the line
between law and tyranny. And so the referee could have waived
the red card — the game was colorful enough —
as well as the penalty kick and the jealous goal post.
Then, brother, your wife would rediscover her love,
as proud as a South American's, and embrace you
with the glowing face of a virgin even after a seventh coupling
and your son would raise his eyes to say
you're the best father. Your friends would treat you
at the bar, singing along with you until dawn
and you'd fall asleep with the sweet feeling that your life
was not lived in vain, on the contrary, it is so very lovely,
and wrong moves don't detract an iota from its beauty.
All this might have taken place if you could read Hebrew poetry
or I had written a poem in the language of the Ashanti.

גלויה אל בת נפשי

לֹא תַאֲמִינִי, זֹאת גְּלוּיָה מִ-Paris
Paris des rêves
פָּרִיז שֶׁל חֲלוֹמוֹת.
מָה, אַתְּ אוֹמֶרֶת לוֹנְדוֹן?
וְהֶחָתוּל הַזֶּה עַל אֶדֶן הַחַלּוֹן
בּוֹהֶה לַנֶּצַח כְּמוֹ הָיָה מִצְרִי עַתִּיק
אֵינוֹ פָּרִיזָאִי? לֹא יִתָּכֵן. אֵין
בְּלוֹנְדוֹן חֲתוּלִים כָּאֵלֶּה. גַּם לֹא
זוּג נֶאֱהָבִים שְׂרוּעִים בַּדֶּשֶׁא – אֵיזֶה חִבּוּק!
הַיְד פַּארְק, אַתְּ אוֹמֶרֶת?
וְיֶרֶק הָאֵשׁ?
אֶפְשָׁר לַחְשֹׁב שֶׁכָּל לִבּוֹ בּוֹעֵר. בְּלוֹנְדוֹן?
וְהַמַּפְרִיחַ כָּאן בּוּעוֹת סַבּוֹן
כְּמוֹ שְׁקָרִים קְטַנִּים וְנוֹצְצִים לְאוֹר הַשֶּׁמֶשׁ –
מִנַּיִן הוּא? וְהַנָּהָר הַזֶּה, אֵפֹר כָּל כָּךְ
עַד שֶׁהָעוֹבֵר אֶל הַגָּדָה מִנֶּגֶד כְּלֹא הָיָה?
וְאֵלֶּה הַיְשֵׁנִים בִּקְצֵה הַמֵּצַח
שְׁמִי יוֹדֵעַ עוֹד מְעַט יוּשְׁטוּ – לְאָן –
לוֹנְדּוֹנִים אוֹ פָּרִיזָאִים, הֵה?
הַתֵּמְזָה? לֹא הַסֵּין? וְאֵיךְ בִּכְלָל
שֶׁאַתְּ עוֹנָה בְּאֶמְצַע שֶׁל כְּתִיבַת גְּלוּיָה
טוֹעֶנֶת אֶת הַהֵפֶךְ, מַכְחִישָׁה אוֹתִי?
רוֹצָה לוֹמַר שֶׁכְּלָל אֵינֶנִּי שָׁם, שֶׁשְּׁנֵינוּ כָּאן
סְמוּכִים, כָּל כָּךְ סְמוּכִים עֲדַיִן
רוֹקְמִים חֲלוֹם?

Postcard to My Soul Mate

You won't believe this — a postcard from Paris —
Paris des rêves,
the Paris of dreams.
What, you say it's London?
And the cat on the window sill
staring forever like an ancient Egyptian
is not Parisian? This can't be. There are no
such cats in London. And no
such pair of lovers lying on the grass — what an embrace!
Hyde Park, you say?
And the fire eater?
It seems like his heart is burning. In London?
And the one blowing soap bubbles
like shiny little lies in sunlight —
where did he come from? And this river, so gray
that a passerby on the other side seems not to exist at all?
And those people sleeping on the edge of the dock
who knows if they'll sail off soon — where to —
are they Londoners or Parisians, eh?
The Thames? Not the Seine? And anyway how can it be
that you answer while I'm writing a postcard
and say just the opposite?
You mean to say I'm not there at all, that we two are here
next to each other, still close,
weaving a dream?

גלויה מאזור חברון

חֶבְרוֹן עִיר עַתִּיקָה מְאֹד.
אַבְרָהָם אָבִינוּ עִם שָׂרָה אִשְׁתּוֹ קְבוּרִים בָּהּ
אוֹמְרִים. דָּבָר קָדוֹשׁ בְּאֶרֶץ הַחַיָּה עַל הַמָּוֶת.
בַּבֹּקֶר אוֹכְלִים בְּחֶבְרוֹן פִּתָּה וְזֵיתִים וְלַבֶּנֶּה בְּשֶׁמֶן זַיִת.
בִּימֵי חַג שׁוֹחֲטִים טָלֶה.
אַנְשֵׁי חֶבְרוֹן אוֹהֲבִים אֶת הַשְּׁחִיטָה.
הַאִם לָמְדוּ אוֹתָהּ מִשִּׁמְעוֹן וְלֵוִי בְּנֵי יַעֲקֹב?
זְמַן רַב
עָבַר מֵאָז.
גַּם אֵרְעוּ כָּל אֵלֶּה בִּשְׁכֶם, שׁוֹנִים הָיוּ פְּנֵי הַדְּבָרִים בְּדוֹרָה, בִּסְבִיבַת חֶבְרוֹן.
בְּדוֹרָה חַסְרִים הַיּוֹם שְׁלֹשָׁה אָבוֹת לְיַלְדֵיהֶם.
אֵזוֹר חֶבְרוֹן יָדוּעַ לִשְׁמְצָה: אֵזוֹר קְשֵׁה עֹרֶף.
בְּ-1929 רָצְחוּ בְּחֶבְרוֹן שִׁשִּׁים וּשְׁמוֹנָה תַּלְמִידֵי יְשִׁיבָה, אִישׁ אִשָּׁה וָטַף.
הוּ קֶבֶר אַבְרָהָם אָבִינוּ (אוֹמְרִים), אָבִינוּ וַאֲבִיהֶם.
הוּ הַחַיָּלִים הַצְּעִירִים הַפּוֹחֲדִים. הוּ הָעֲשָׂרָה בְּמַרְס 1998.
כִּמְעַט יָרֵחַ מָלֵא, אַךְ הָיָה עוֹד אוֹר יוֹם. פּוֹעֲלִים מֵאֵזוֹר חֶבְרוֹן
נָסְעוּ הַבַּיְתָה. בִּכְבִישׁ חֶבְרוֹן, בְּתַרְקוּמְיָא, יֵשׁ מַחְסוֹם.
לְיַד הַמַּחְסוֹם עָמְדוּ חַיָּלִים. נַהַג הַמְּכוֹנִית אִבֵּד שְׁלִיטָה. מְכוֹנִיתוֹ
דָּהֲרָה אֶל הַמַּחְסוֹם. מְפַקֵּד הַמַּחְסוֹם
נִפְגַּע וְנֶהְדַּף לַכִּוּוּן הַנֶּגְדִּי.
יֵשׁ גַּם גִּרְסָה אַחֶרֶת.
חֲבֵרָיו סָבְרוּ כִּי רוֹצִים לְדָרְסוֹ.
קָשֶׁה לָדַעַת לְמִי לְהַאֲמִין וְלָמָּה.
פָּתְחוּ בְּאֵשׁ כְּהֶרֶף-עַיִן.
לְפִי הַהוֹרָאוֹת. לְפִי הַפְּקֻדּוֹת.
בְּאֵיזוֹ מְהִירוּת זֶה מִתְרַחֵשׁ. בְּאֵיזוֹ מְהִירוּת
פּוֹשְׁטִים צוּרָה, הוֹפְכִים לְאַחֵר:
בְּלִי נִיעַ, פְּנֵי גֶּבֶס, עֵינֵי זְכוּכִית.
אוֹ אַחַר כָּךְ זְרוֹעוֹת רְפוּיוֹת, שׁוּב מִלִּים בַּפֶּה, לֹא צְעָקוֹת.

Postcard from the Hebron Area

Hebron is a very ancient city.
Our father Abraham is buried there with his wife Sarah
they say. Very holy for a land that lives off death.
In Hebron they eat pita and olives and white cheese in olive oil in the morning.
On holidays they sacrifice a lamb.
The people of Hebron love the slaughter.
Did they learn this from Jacob's sons Shimon and Levi?
It's been
a long time.
And those things happened in Nablus; it's different in Dura, around Hebron.
In Dura today, three fathers are lost to their children now.
The Hebron area has a bad reputation: it's a stiff-necked place.
In 1929, sixty-eight yeshiva students, women and children were murdered
        in Hebron.
Oh tomb of Abraham our father (they say), our father and theirs.
Oh the young, frightened soldiers. Oh, March 10, 1998.
The moon nearly full, but it was still daylight. Workers from the Hebron area
were riding home. On the Hebron Road, at Tarkumia, there is a checkpoint.
Soldiers stood at the checkpoint. The driver of the car lost control. The car
rushed toward the checkpoint. The checkpoint commander was hurt
and hurled in the opposite direction.
There is also another version.
The soldiers thought the driver wanted to run him over.
It's hard to know whom to believe and what.
They opened fire in the blink of an eye.
According to instructions. According to orders.
How fast it happens. How fast
one loses shape, becomes something else:
immobile, a plaster face, glass eyes.
Or limp arms afterwards, words in the mouth once again instead of screams.

אֶתְמוֹל עוֹד פָּתָה וְזֵיתִים וְלִפְנוֹת בֹּקֶר אוּלַי מְשֻׁגָּל.
אֶתְמוֹל עוֹד לוֹגְרִיתְמִים, הִסְטוֹרְיָה, נְעָרוֹת עַל שְׂפַת הַיָּם. וּפֶתַע
הַכְּבִישׁ מְזֻהַם כְּתָמִים אֲדֻמִּים. הַיָּרֵחַ כִּמְעַט מָלֵא, לָבָן כְּעֶצֶם.
הִתְרוֹצְצוּת אָנֶה וָאָנָה, קְרִיאוֹת, הָלְאָה עִם זֶה, אַחַר כָּךְ הָאֲבָנִים.
הַאִם מִתְרַבּוֹת הָאֲבָנִים? לְאַט לְאַט, אֵין לַעֲצֹר, פָּרוֹת וְרַבּוֹת הָאֲבָנִים.

Yesterday more pita and olives and perhaps sex before dawn.
Yesterday more logarithms, history, girls on the beach. And suddenly
the road is spotted with red. The moon nearly full, white as bone.
Running to and fro, shouts, onward, afterwards the stones.
Do stones reproduce? Slowly, there's no stopping it, the stones are fruitful
    and multiply.

גלויה מווינה

זְרוֹעַ שְׁלוּחָה אֶפְשָׁר גַּם לְהוֹרִיד
מֵעַל-יָד – לְהַרְפּוֹת.
פֶּה מָלֵא צְרָחוֹת מְסֻגָּל גַּם לְדַבֵּר
צְוָחוֹת שִׂמְחָה עֲשׂוּיוֹת לְהִתְגַּלְגֵּל בִּשְׂחוֹק.
לֹא בְּהֶכְרֵחַ יֵשׁ לְנַקּוֹת מִדְרָכוֹת בְּמִבְרֶשֶׁת-שִׁנַּיִם
וְאַף-עַל-פִּי-כֵן וִינָה עִיר יָפָה וּנְקִיָּה לְמִשְׁעִי
בַּעֲלַת עָבָר עָשִׁיר. הַרְבֵּה מוּזִיקָאִים
הִתְגּוֹרְרוּ בָּהּ, שַׂחְקָנִים, סוֹפְרִים לָרֹב.
עִיר שֶׁיֵּשׁ לָהּ בַּמֶּה לְהִתְפָּאֵר.
בַּהֶלְדֶנְפְּלָץ מְקַשְׁקְשִׁים הַדְּרוֹרִים
הַהֲמִיָּה הָעֲמוּמָה מְקוֹרָהּ בַּתְּנוּעָה הָעֵרָה.
קָרְבָּן אֵינוֹ צָרִיךְ לְהִתְבַּיֵּשׁ כִּי
הָיָה קָרְבָּן. גַּם הַדָּנוּבָּה
לָאו דַּוְקָא כְּחֻלָּה.
הַטּוֹב בְּמוּבָן מְסֻיָּם מַשְׁמִים, רָשַׁם קַפְקָא
וּלְלֹא נִחוּמִים. הֱיִי שָׁלוֹם.

Postcard from Vienna

A raised arm may be lowered
a salute — withdrawn.
A mouth filled with shrieks is also capable of speaking.
Wild shouts may turn into laughter.
It isn't absolutely necessary to clean sidewalks with toothbrushes.
Yet Vienna is beautiful, a spotlessly clean city
with a rich past. Many musicians
lived there, actors, a lot of authors.
A city with much to be proud of.
On the Heldenplatz the sparrows chatter,
the traffic hums.
A hangman doesn't have to be ashamed because he was
a hangman. And the Danube
is not really blue.
In a certain sense goodness is boring, Kafka wrote,
and without consolations. Be seeing you.

גלויה מפרשבורג-בראטיסלווה

בְּרַטִיסְלַוָה הִיא פְּרֶשְׁבּוּרג הִיא פּוֹז'וֹנִי.
בִּשְׁבִילִי הִיא פְּרֶשְׁבּוּרג.
מוֹרִי, מַר ווּרם מֵהָעֲמָמִי
הוֹצִיא מִמְּגֵרָתוֹ אֶת תַּצְלוּם הַכִּתָּה וְהִצְבִּיעַ:
זֶה הָיָה נָאצִי וְגַם זֶה וְזֶה. הַהוּא
הָיָה אַכְזָרִי בִּמְיֻחָד. הַלָּה נָפַל בְּרוּסְיָה
וְאוֹתוֹ גֵּרְשׁוּ. מִי מֵהַתַּלְמִידִים הַיְּהוּדִים
שָׂרַד וָחַי – אֵינִי יוֹדֵעַ.
פְּרֶשְׁבּוּרג הָיְתָה עִיר תְּלַת-לְשׁוֹנִית. הַלָּשׁוֹן הָרְבִיעִית
הִיא הַשְּׁתִיקָה.
הַאִם הָיוּ פַּעַם גְּבוּלוֹת לָרֵעַ?
פְּרֶשְׁבּוּרג שׁוֹכֶנֶת לְיַד הַדָּנוּבָּה, בְּקֶצֶה שְׁלוּחוֹת הַקַּרְפָּטִים.
בְּקִרְבַת הַקָּתֶדְרָלָה עָמַד בֵּית-הַכְּנֶסֶת שֶׁל הַנֵּיאוֹלוֹגִים
בְּסִגְנוֹן מָאוּרִי כָּלְשֶׁהוּ. לְמַטָּה שְׂרוּעָה כִּכַּר הַדָּגִים
לְמַעְלָה הִתְחִיל רְחוֹב הַיְּהוּדִים. הַדָּנוּבָּה זוֹרֶמֶת כְּמוֹ תָּמִיד.
אֲנִי זָקֵן. אֵינִי יָכוֹל לְהִתְקַדֵּם אֶלָּא לְאַט.
בִּפְרֶשְׁבּוּרג נוֹלַדְתִּי. הָיוּ לִי אֵם, אָב וְאָחוֹת.
הָיְתָה לִי, כְּמִדְּמֶה, יַלְדוּת קְטַנָּה מְאֻשֶּׁרֶת בִּפְרֶשְׁבּוּרג.
פַּעַם קָפְאָה הַדָּנוּבָּה כָּל-כֻּלָּהּ.
הַקֶּלְטִים בָּנוּ כָּאן מִבְצָר, וְגַם נְסִיכֵי
מוֹרַבְיָה רַבָּתִי. הָרוֹמָאִים קָרְאוּ לַמָּקוֹם
פּוֹזוֹנְיוּם. זֹאת עִיר בָּאָה-בַּיָּמִים.
כֹּה בָּאָה-בַּיָּמִים עַד שֶׁאֵינֶי יוֹדְעָה עוֹד.
לְהִתְרָאוֹת, אֲהוּבָה, קָשֶׁה לְשַׁעֵר.

Postcard from Pressburg-Bratislava

Bratislava is Pressburg is Pozsony.
For me it is Pressburg.
My teacher from the grade school
took a class photo from his drawer and pointed:
this one was a Nazi and these two also. That one
was especially cruel. This one died in Russia
and this one was deported. Which Jewish students
survived and are still alive — I don't know.
Pressburg was a trilingual city. The fourth language
is silence.
Have there ever been limits to evil?
Pressburg lies next to the Danube, at the edge of a Carpathian range.
Near the cathedral was the Neologists' synagogue in a sort of Moorish style.
Fish Market Square stretches out below
and the Street of the Jews began above it. The Danube flows as always.
I'm old. I can only move forward slowly.
I was born in Pressburg. I had a mother, a father and a sister.
I had, it seems to me, a modest, happy childhood in Pressburg.
Once the entire Danube froze.
The Celts built a fortress here, as did the princes of
greater Moravia. The Romans called the place
Possonium. A very old city,
so old I don't know it any more.
Farewell, my love, it's hard to imagine.

גלויה מששטין: מדורות סתיו

שֶׁשְׁטִין, סָפֵק עֲיָרָה סָפֵק כְּפָר, קְרוֹבָה לִגְבוּל מוֹרַבְיָה.
מְקוֹם עֲלִיָּה לָרֶגֶל שֶׁל נוֹצְרִים, עִם כְּנֵסִיָּה גְּדוֹלָה וּמְפֹאֶרֶת
עֲצֵי עַרְמוֹן בַּחֲזִיתָהּ, מִנְזָר שֶׁל סִילֶזְיָאנִים
קְיוֹסְקִים גְּדוֹשִׁים פִּסְלֵי קְדוֹשִׁים וּמַמְתַּקִּים בִּימֵי חַג וְיָרִיד.
בַּזִּכָּרוֹן אֵין זְמַן עָבָר.
כִּכַּר הַשּׁוּק כְּבָר מְכֻסָּה בֶּטוֹן, הַמְּתוֹפֵף תּוֹפֵף עַל תֹּף הַפַּח
מַכְרִיז בְּקוֹל חֲדָשׁוֹת שְׁנַת 34 אוֹ 36, מִכָּל מָקוֹם בְּטֶרֶם
שֶׁשְׁטִין נֶהֶפְכָה. לִפְנֵי
יוּנִי 42.
אָז נֶאֶלְמָה דָּם שֶׁשְׁטִין, לֹא הוֹצִיאָה הֶגֶה כַּאֲשֶׁר
הַמְּתִינָה הָרַכֶּבֶת – מִשְּׂמֹאל לַכְּבִישׁ, לְיַד בֵּיתוֹ שֶׁל
ד"ר נוֹבוֹמֶסְקִי אִם בָּאתָ מִכִּכַּר הַשּׁוּק שָׁם עוֹמֵד
הַבַּיִת שֶׁל הַסַּבִּים. הוֹרַי וַאֲחוֹתִי שׁוֹהִים אֶצְלָם
(הַאִם הוֹלְכִים הֵם עַל מִזְוְדוֹתֵיהֶם בָּרֶגֶל אֶל הַתַּחֲנָה, הַאִם עוֹדָם
מְפַנִים אֶת רֹאשָׁם לְאָחוֹר לִרְאוֹת אֶת עֵין הָאוֹכְרָה שֶׁלַבַּיִת? – (הַיּוֹם אֵין לְהַכִּיר) – וְנָסְעָה צָפוֹנָה.
יִשּׁוּב קָטָן סְתָמִי, לַמְרוֹת פְּאֵר הַכְּנֵסִיָּה, מַשְׂמִים בְּסַךְ הַכֹּל. לְנֶשֶׁם בּוֹ
אִי אֶפְשָׁר. הַכֹּל עָשָׁן. לֹא כְּלוּם לְהִתְבּוֹנֵן. אַף לֹא אֶחָד
לִקְשֹׁר שִׂיחָה. לֹא כְּלוּם לִכְתֹּב עָלָיו.

16

Postcard from Šaštin: Autumn Bonfires

Šaštin, a town or maybe a village, close to the Moravian border.
A place of Christian pilgrimage, with a large, grand church
fronted by chestnut trees, a Silesian monastery
and kiosks bursting with statues of saints and candy on feast and market days.
In memory there is no past tense.
The market square now covered in concrete, a drummer beats on a tin drum
announcing the news of '34 or '36, before
Šaštin turned upside down. Before
June '42.
Then Šaštin was struck dumb, didn't utter a sound
when the train waited —
on the left side of the street, next to Dr. Novomesky's house
if you were coming from the market square near
the house of my grandparents, my parents and sister staying there
(are they walking with their suitcases to the station, do they still
turn their heads around to see the ochre eye of the house? — (unrecognizable
          today) — and traveled north.
Just a small place, despite the cathedral's splendor, boring all in all. Impossible
to breathe. Everything is smoke. Nothing to see. No one
to talk to. Nothing to write about.

גלויה מצירִיך

צירִיך מִתְחַכֶּכֶת בַּצירִיכְבֶּרְג.
צירִיך אֵינָה אוֹהֶבֶת דְּגוּגִים מִתַּחַת לַפַּרְוָה.
צירִיך אוֹהֶבֶת סֵדֶר, חֲרוּצָה הִיא, לָאו דַּוְקָא מַסְבִּירָה פָּנִים
וּבַעֲלַת לֵב חַם בִּמְיֻחָד, אַך יְשָׁרָה, הוֹגֶנֶת, אַם פָּחוֹת
וְאַם יוֹתֵר. וּמִי אֵינוּ חוֹשֵׁב עַל רֶוַח? לֹא כָּל הַנּוֹצֵץ
זָהָב. צירִיך אֵינָה נוֹצֶצֶת. הִיא פִּקַּחַת, לֹא אוֹהֶבֶת
לְנַחֵשׁ, לִפְתֹּר חִידוֹת. עֲבָדוֹת אוֹהֶבֶת צירִיך: אֶת הַבַּנְהוֹפְשְׁטְרַסֶה
וְהַפְּרָאוּאֶנְמִינְסְטֶר, צוּם שְׁטוֹרְכֶן, עוֹד תָּמִיד אוֹרְחִים, לֹא תָּמִיד
מְשׁוֹרְרִים, הַבַּיִת שֶׁבּוֹ בִּיכְנֵר מֵת וְלֶנִין דָּר. הַקּוּנְסְטְהָאוּס. אִין
דֶּר אַיְ 37. הָאֵיטְלִיבֶּרְג.
אָדָם בָּא בַּיָּמִים אַם לַדְּבָרִים יִקְרָא בִּשְׁמָם – דַּיּוֹ.
מִלָּה אַחַת – חַיִּים שְׁלֵמִים.
וְלֹא-עַל-נְקַלָּה תַּקְפִּיד עַל סֵדֶר בָּעִיר סְדוּרָה זֹאת כַּאֲשֶׁר
הִיא זִכָּרוֹן. הַזִּכָּרוֹן הֲלֹא
מֵגִיחַ פֶּתַע, מִתְחַבֵּא, זוֹנֵק. קָשֶׁה הוּא לְרִסּוֹן.
בַּזִּכָּרוֹן נֶאֱלָם הַמָּוֶת דָּם, אֵין לוֹ רְשׁוּת דִּבּוּר. אֲבָל
גַּם צירִיך הִשְׁתַּנְּתָה. אֲנַחְנוּ
הִשְׁתַּנֵּינוּ רַב מִמֶּנָּה. צירִיך לְבַסּוֹף הִיא צירִיך.
לֹא תְשׁוּשָׁה, לֹא מַבִּיטָה אֲחוֹרָה
בְּמִין סָפֵק. אֵין הָאֲגַם נוֹטֵשׁ אוֹתָהּ
גַּם אַם כֻּלּוֹ כְּנָפַיִם בְּיוֹם שֶׁמֶשׁ.
כִּמְעַט שֶׁכַחְתִּי: בְּצירִיך עוֹד הָיִינוּ כָּאן
כֻּלָּנוּ, הֵסַבְנוּ לְשֻׁלְחָן אֶחָד לְפַת-עַרְבִית
אִישׁ אִישׁ, כֻּלָּנוּ.

Postcard from Zurich

Zurich rubs against the Zurichberg.
Zurich doesn't like being tickled under its fur.
Zurich likes order, it's hardworking, not necessarily welcoming
or particularly warmhearted, but direct, fair, more
or less so. And who doesn't think about profit? Not everything that glitters
is gold. Zurich doesn't glitter. It's sober, doesn't like
to guess, to solve riddles. Zurich likes facts, the Bahnhofstrasse,
the Fraumuenster, zum Storchen, guests even more, not always
poets, the house where Buechner died, and Lenin lived. The Kunsthaus.
In der Ey 37, the Uetliberg.
If an old man calls things by their names — that's enough.
One word — an entire life.
And it is not easy to insist upon order in this orderly city which is
already a memory. A memory that surely
emerges suddenly, hides, leaps. Hard to restrain.
In memory, death is struck dumb. It doesn't have the right to speak. But
Zurich has also changed. We
have changed more. Zurich is just Zurich in the end.
It isn't exhausted. It doesn't look back
with a sort of uncertainty. The lake doesn't abandon the city
even when it's all wings on a sunny day.
I almost forgot: in Zurich we were all still here
together, we sat around one table for our evening meal
each one, all of us.

גלויה מלונדון

אֶת הַגְּלוּיָה הַזֹּאת אֲנִי כּוֹתֵב מִלּוֹנְדּוֹן.
לוֹנְדּוֹן גְּדוֹלָה מִדַּי בִּשְׁבִילִי.
אֲנִי מִסְתַּפֵּק בַּנֶּשִׁיוֹנָל גָּאלֶרִי.
הַנֶּשְׁיוֹנָל גָּאלֶרִי גְּדוֹלָה מִדַּי בִּשְׁבִילִי. אֲנִי מִסְתַּפֵּק
בַּדְּיוֹקָן הָעַצְמִי שֶׁל רֶמְבְּרַנְדְט בִּהְיוֹתוֹ
בֶּן שִׁשִּׁים וְשָׁלֹשׁ. הַתַּאֲרִיךְ הוּא 1669
שְׁנַת חַיָּיו הָאַחֲרוֹנָה. הַיּוֹם אֲנִי
גָּדוֹל מִמֶּנּוּ בְּאַחַת-עֶשְׂרֵה שָׁנִים. אַךְ "הַתְּמוּנָה
לֹא יָכְלָה לִהְיוֹת צְנוּעָה יוֹתֵר, הַחִקּוּר הָעַצְמִי
לֹא נִמְרָץ יוֹתֵר," כָּתוּב בַּקָּטָלוֹג, פְּרִי עֵטוֹ
– כִּלְשׁוֹן שֶׁל פַּעַם – שֶׁל מַיְיקְל לִיוִי, וַאֲנִי מַמְשִׁיךְ
(אֲנִי אוֹהֵב מוּבָאוֹת, אֶפְשָׁר לְהִסְתַּמֵּךְ עֲלֵיהֶן
בָּאִים לִידֵי שִׂיחָה, גַּם לַאֲחֵרִים יֵשׁ לוֹמַר
נוֹצֶרֶת מֵעֵין פּוֹלִיפוֹנְיָה): "בַּפּוֹרְטְרֶטִים מִשְּׁנוֹתָיו
הָאַחֲרוֹנוֹת הוּא מַצִּיג אֶת עַצְמוֹ כְּצַיָּר וּכְאָדָם הַמִּתְדַּיֵּן
עִם הָעוֹלָם כְּמִתְגָּרֶה בּוֹ אוֹ נִכְנָע לוֹ וּמֻתָּר. בַּדְּיוֹקָן
הַזֶּה, דּוֹמֶה, אֵין הָעוֹלָם אֶלָּא אֵי-שָׁם בָּרֶקַע." לוֹנְדּוֹן
הָעִיר הַפּוֹלִיפוֹנִית שֶׁאֲנִי מַכִּיר, כֻּלָּה בָּרֶקַע.
טְרָפַלְגָּר סְקְוֵּיר כִּמְעַט בְּלִי קוֹל, סֶנְט גֵ'יְמְס פַּרְק
עִם צִפֳּרֵי הַמַּיִם וְהַקְיוֹסְק הַגָּדוֹל, וֶסְטְמִינְסְטֶר
הַפַּרְלָמֶנְט וְצַ'רִינְג קְרוֹס, סֶנְט פּוֹל, הַטֵּאָטְר
אַחַר-כָּךְ הַתַּמְזָה בְּכִוּוּן לַיָּם – בָּרֶקַע. הַמִּזְחִים הַזְּעִירִים
הַבִּנְיָנִים, הָאֳנִיּוֹת וְהַסִּירוֹת, גְּרִינִיץ', הַזְּמַן הַמְּדֻיָּק.
הָעֵינַיִם הַלָּלוּ
הָעֵינַיִם הַקְּשׁוּבוֹת, הָעֲיֵפוֹת, הַיְּדוּעוֹת הַלָּלוּ
רוֹאוֹת כָּל זֶה וְלֹא רוֹאוֹת. רַק קְנָווּד הָאוֹס רוֹמֵז עוֹד מֵרָחוֹק
וְהַדְּיוֹקָן, תֵּשַׁע שָׁנִים צָעִיר יוֹתֵר, טַבְלַת צְבָעִים בַּיָּד, וּבְמַבָּט דּוֹמֶה.
(הַאִם הוּא מַאֲזִין לַמְּנַגֶּנֶת שֶׁל וֶרְמֶר?)

20

Postcard from London

I'm writing this postcard from London.
London is too big for me.
The National Gallery is enough.
The National Gallery is too big for me.
The self-portrait of Rembrandt at sixty-three is enough. The date is 1669,
the last year of his life. Today I am
eleven years older than he was. But "the picture
could not be more modest, the self-examination
less intense," the catalog says, "from the pen of" —
as they used to say — Michael Levey, and I go on
(I like quotations, you can count on them
to create conversation, others also have something to say,
a sort of polyphony): "In portraits from the last
years of his life he presents himself as a painter and a person contending
with a world that either provokes him or surrenders and lets him go. In this
portrait, it seems, the world is somewhere in the background." London,
the polyphonic city I know, is all background.
Nearly soundless Trafalgar Square, St. James Park
with its water birds and large kiosk, Westminster
and the Parliament and Charing Cross, St. Paul, the Tower
then the Thames toward the sea — in the background. The tiny docks
the buildings, the boats and ships, Greenwich, the exact time.
These eyes
these attentive, tired, knowing eyes
see it all and don't see. Kenwood House is in the distance,
its portrait nine years younger, a palette of colors in his hand, and a similar look.
(Is he listening to Vermeer's music student?)

"הַצֶּבַע הֵנַח בְּחַסְכָנוּת גְּאוֹנִית."
הַיָּדַיִם שְׁלוּבוֹת, אוֹחֲזוֹת זוֹ בָּזוֹ בְּרִפְיוֹן.
שׁוּב אֵינָן רוֹצוֹת לִתְפֹּס דָּבָר אוֹ לְהַחֲזִיק בּוֹ.
לוֹנְדּוֹן רְחוֹקָה, אֵינָהּ אֶלָּא גְּלוּיָה, הֵיי שָׁלוֹם.

"The paint is applied with brilliant economy."
Arms crossed, clasping each other loosely.
They don't want to grasp or hold anything any more.
London is far away, nothing but a postcard, farewell.

גלויה מירושלים

יְרוּשָׁלַיִם יָצְאָה מִירוּשָׁלַיִם וְהִסְתַּלְקָה לָהּ.
זֶה שָׁם לְמַעְלָה בָּאֲוִיר, הֲלֹא לֹא יִתָּכֵן שֶׁזֹּאת יְרוּשָׁלַיִם?

Postcard from Jerusalem

Jerusalem left Jerusalem and ran away.
That thing up there, surely it can't be Jerusalem?

השגרירים

אֵינִי יוֹדֵעַ כֵּיצַד לְהַתְחִיל.
הֲרֵי הָעִקָּר הוּא הַגֻּלְגֹּלֶת.
מַדּוּעַ דַּוְקָא מֵהַזָּוִית הַזֹּאת?

הִנֵּה, שְׁנֵי גְּבָרִים חֲסָנִים, כִּבְנֵי אַרְבָּעִים.
הָאֶחָד מְכֻנָּס בְּעַצְמוֹ בְּמִדַּת-מָה.
הָאַחֵר נִצָּב בְּרַגְלַיִם פְּשׂוּקוֹת,
רֶגֶל אַחַת בְּעִגּוּל בְּרִצְפַּת הַשַּׁיִשׁ
כְּבַחוּג הַשָּׁמַיִם.
אַדַּרְתּוֹ עֲטוּרָה פַּרְוָה יְקָרָה,
שַׁרְווּלֶיהָ הַלוּלַת אֲרִיגִים.
הַכֹּחַ כָּבוּשׁ בּוֹ כַּבָּרָק בַּגַּרְעִין
קֹדֶם לְהַבְקָעָה.
שְׁנֵי שַׁגְרִירִים, אֲנִי קוֹרֵא,
בַּעֲלֵי שֵׁם צָרְפָתִי, ז'אן דֶה דֶנְטְוִיל
וְז'וֹרז' דֶה סֶלְב.
גַּם הַמְהַרְהָר יוֹדֵעַ אֶת עֶרְכּוֹ.
וּמַה זֶּה בְּמֶלְכְּסָן, בָּאֶמְצַע?

הֵם נִשְׁעָנִים עַל מִין כּוֹנָנִית מְכֻסָּה
שָׁטִיחַ פַּרְסִי אָדֹם, עָלָיו מֻצָּגִים
מַכְשִׁירִים שׁוֹנִים, מַכְשִׁירֵי נְטוֹת,
אִם אֵינֶנִּי טוֹעֶה, מְחוּגָה, קֻבִּיָּה,
אוֹ אִצְטַגְנִינוּת.
גְּלוֹבּוּס יְפֵהפֶה עוֹמֵד שָׁם.
וּבַמַּדָּף הַנָּמוּךְ – קַתְרוֹס וְסֵפֶר שֶׁדַּפָּיו פְּתוּחִים:
הֵם הוּמָנִיסְטִים, שְׁנֵי הַשַּׁגְרִירִים הַלָּלוּ, אוֹ מִכָּל מָקוֹם
מְאוֹהֲבֵי הָאָמָּנֻיּוֹת הַיָּפוֹת.
הוֹלְבַּיין הַצָּעִיר צִיְּרָם עַל עֵץ אַלּוֹן בְּרֵאשִׁית הַמֵּאָה הַשֵּׁשׁ-עֶשְׂרֵה.

The Ambassadors

I don't know where to begin.
The main thing is the skull. But
why this angle?

Here are two sturdy men, about forty.
One is absorbed in himself to some extent.
The other stands with his legs apart,
a foot inside the circle on the marble floor
as though within the vault of heaven.
His coat collared in expensive fur,
its sleeves richly embroidered,
his strength suppressed like flashes in an atom
before it breaks open.
The two ambassadors, I read,
have French names, Jean de Dinteville,
and Georges de Selve.
The thoughtful one also knows his worth.
And what is that on a slant, in the middle?

They are leaning on a kind of chest
covered with a red Persian rug, upon which
different instruments are displayed, navigational tools,
if I'm not mistaken, a compass, a cube,
astrological devices.
A beautiful globe
and on the lower shelf — a lute and a book whose pages are open.
They are humanists, these ambassadors,
or at least lovers of fine art.
Holbein the Younger painted them on oak at the beginning of the
        16th century.

מַדּוּעַ מַבִּיטִים בִּי הַשְּׁנַיִם עַל רֶקַע הַוִּילוֹן הַיָּרֹק,
הַשַּׁגְרִירִים הַלָּלוּ עִם הַשֵּׁמוֹת הַזָּרִים,
מַדּוּעַ מַבִּיטִים בִּי בִּכְבֵד-רֹאשׁ כָּזֶה,
אֵינָם מַשְׁפִּילִים מַבָּט אַף לֹא לְהֶרֶף-עַיִן,
שְׁמוּרוֹתֵיהֶם קָפְאוּ,
וְאֵינָם אוֹמְרִים דָּבָר?

בְּאַחַת פָּרַץ הָאָבִיב.
תּוֹךְ שָׁבוּעַ יָמִים הוֹרִיקוּ הָעֵצִים כֻּלָּם.
צִבְעֵי הַפְּרִיחָה נִזְדַּוְּגוּ, נִתְפָּרְדוּ, נִזְדַּוְּגוּ,
צָעֲקוּ מִשִּׂמְחָה.
הַשָּׁמַיִם בָּרָק.
אִם מִסְתַּכְּלִים מִצַּד יָמִין רוֹאִים בְּבֵרוּר:
גֻּלְגֹּלֶת עֲנָק, מְעֻוֶּתֶת.
עֶצֶם עֲצוּמָה שֶׁתַּחֲנֹק כָּל גָּרוֹן.
רַק מֵהַזָּוִית הַזֹּאת הִיא נִכֶּרֶת
אִם תַּעֲמֹד מִמּוּל אֵין זֶה אֶלָּא
מַשֶּׁהוּ לֹא מוּבָן.
אֵיזֶה מִין כֶּתֶם צְהַבְהַב מֵטִיל צֵל.
טֵרוּף שָׁקֵט בְּאֵין מִלִּים מַשְׁחִית אֶת הַתְּמוּנָה.

28

Why do these two, framed by the green curtain, look at me,
these ambassadors with strange names,
why do they look at me so seriously
never letting their glances falter for a moment,
their eyelids frozen,
and never say a word?

Spring blossomed all at once,
within a week all the trees were green
the colors coupled, separated, coupled,
shouted with joy,
the sky flashed.
If you stand on the right you will clearly see
a giant distorted skull,
a huge bone that would choke any throat,
noticeable only from this angle.
If you stand opposite
it is just something unrecognizable,
some kind of a yellowish spot casting a shadow.
A wordless madness slaughters the picture.

הנערים

תָּמִיד הֵם מְחַיְּכִים הַנְּעָרִים הַלָּלוּ
וְהַגְּבָרִים שֶׁאֵין לָהֶם גִּיל.
אֲפִלּוּ אֵינָם אֶלָּא טוֹרְסוֹ
אַתָּה מְדַמֶּה לִרְאוֹת אֶת הַחִיּוּךְ עַל פְּנֵיהֶם.
הֵם מְחַיְּכִים פְּנִימָה אֶל תּוֹךְ עַצְמָם.
נְקֻדַּת כָּבְדָּם מַשֶּׁהוּ מִתַּחַת לַלֵּב.
הֵם הוֹלְכִים בְּנוּחָם וְנָחִים בְּלֶכְתָּם
שׁוֹמְרֵי-מִפְתָּן אֵלֶּה שֶׁל הַחֲלוֹמוֹת.

בְּיוֹם רִאשׁוֹן בַּבֹּקֶר יָצָא הַבֵּן אֶת הָאָרֶץ.
פָּנָיו לַדְּרָכִים הַמַּפְלִיגוֹת,
לַמַּיִם הַמִּתְפַּלְּגִים תַּחְתָּיו.
הוּא יִפְנֶה לְכָאן וּלְכָאן.
אֵין לָדַעַת מָתַי יָשׁוּב.
בַּת שְׂחוֹק חֲבוּיָה מִבַּעַד לְפָנָיו.
מְהַלְּכוֹת אַגָּדוֹת לְמִינֵיהֶן.

עֵינֵיהֶם הָרֵיקוֹת רוֹאוֹת גַּם בַּחֹשֶׁךְ.
מִפְּנֵי עִוְרוֹנָן אֵין מָנוֹס.
הֵן זוֹכְרוֹת אֶת אִיגֵאוּס, הַמִּפְרָשׂ הַשָּׁחֹר.
יְדֵיהֶם קְמוּצוֹת כָּלְשֶׁהוּ, צְמוּדוֹת לְגוּפָם.
"חַיִּים הֵם מָוֶת וּמָוֶת גַּם הוּא חַיִּים"

The Youths

They are always smiling, these youths
and the ageless men.
Even when they are only torsos
you imagine a smile on their faces,
inward at themselves.
The center of gravity is somewhere under the heart.
They walk while resting, rest while walking,
these entrance guards of dreams.

On Sunday morning the son left the country
heading in the wake of sails,
water splitting underneath.
He will turn this way and that.
There's no telling when he'll return.
A small smile is hidden inside his face.
All kinds of legends are spreading.

Their empty eyes see also in the dark.
There is nothing to be done about their blindness.
They remember Aegeus, the black sail.
Their hands are somewhat fisted
close to their bodies.
"Life is death and death is also life"

החיוך

תָּמִיד הֵם מְחַיְּכִים הַנְּעָרִים הַלָּלוּ
וְהַגְּבָרִים שֶׁאֵין לָהֶם גִּיל.
אֲפִלּוּ אֵינָם אֶלָּא טוֹרְסוֹ
אֵין הַחִיּוּךְ סָר מֵעֲלֵיהֶם.
הֵם הוֹלְכִים בְּנוּחָם וְנָחִים בְּלֶכְתָּם
שׁוֹמְרֵי-מִפְתָּן אֵלֶּה שֶׁל הַחֲלוֹמוֹת.

הַכִּכָּר בַּחוּץ – מִשְׁכַּב חַמָּה.
בָּתֵּי הַקָּפֶה בַּחֲצִי הַגֹּרֶן הוֹמִים מֵאָדָם.
אוֹהֲבִים צוֹחֲקִים מְמַזְּגִים אֶת פְּנֵיהֶם.

גַּם פָּרָשׁ בֵּינֵיהֶם. הַסּוּס אָבַד.
רְאוּי לִזְכֹּר אַף אֶת הָאִישׁ הַשּׁוֹכֵחַ לְאָן מוֹלִיכָה הַדֶּרֶךְ.
מָוֶת הוּא אֲשֶׁר רוֹאִים הָעֵרִים, אֲבָל בַּשֵּׁנָה

"חַבֵּק אוֹתִי קְצָת וְאַל תַּחֲלֹם שָׁם,
בּוֹא וְנַשֵּׁק אוֹתִי, חַיָּכָן אֶחָד!"

The Smile

They are always smiling, these youths
and the ageless men.
Even when they are only torsos
they never lose their smiles.
They walk while resting, rest while walking,
these entrance guards of dreams.

The square outside — a sunbath.
Crowded coffeehouses in a half-circle.
Lovers laughing, faces joined.

And a rider among them. The horse lost.
Worth remembering the one who forgot where he is going.
The ones who are awake see death, but while sleeping

"Hold me a little and don't dream,
come and kiss me, smiling one!"

ההורדה מהצלב

שַׂק קֶמַח עָבֵשׁ, נֹאד
לָבָן, נָפוּחַ, הַמּוֹשִׁיעַ
מוּרָד מִן הָעֵץ הַמֻּכְתָּם, הָרֹאשׁ –
לֹא-רֹאשׁ נָפוּל, שָׁמוּט כְּמוֹ
כַּדּוּר-פּוֹרֵחַ זָעִיר
חֲסַר אֲוִיר. אֶחָד אוֹחֵז בִּזְרוֹעַ
הַבֻּבָּה הַכְּעוּרָה הַזֹּאת,
נוֹעֵץ בָּהּ עֵינַיִם בְּתִמָּהוֹן,
חֶמְלָה וָפַחַד. אֲחֵרִים נוֹשְׂאִים
וְנוֹתְנִים וְלוֹקְחִים בְּפָנִים
תּוֹעִים בֵּין מַעְלָה וּמַטָּה.
שָׁמֵן עָטוּר מִצְנֶפֶת
עוֹמֵד וּמִתְבּוֹנֵן
מְרֻצֶּה מִכִּרְסוֹ הַחַיָּה שֶׁל עַצְמוֹ.
עַל רֶקַע הָרָקִיעַ הָאָפֵל
מִתְכּוֹפֵף אֶחָד, מַנִּיחַ
לְאַט לַסָּדִין לִצְנֹחַ.
הַכֹּל אָפֵל סָבִיב. גַּם הָעֵצִים.
רַק הַגּוּפָה זוֹהֶרֶת.

לֹא. לֹא כָּךְ. עוֹד פַּעַם. מֵהַתְחָלָה.
בָּשָׂר לָבָן וָרֹד, כְּמִדְּמֶה,
חַי, נוֹשֵׁם, מֵנִיעַ זְרוֹעוֹת,
אֲפִלּוּ אוֹהֵב. מִחוּץ לַמִּסְגֶּרֶת,
יֵשׁ לַשַּׁעַר יַנִּיחוּהוּ בַּבּוֹר.
יַנִּיחוּהוּ? יָנוּחַ? מְנוּחַת עוֹלָמִים.
לֹא. לֹא כָּךְ.

The Descent from the Cross

Moldy sack of flour, swollen
white wineskin, the savior
is removed from the spotted wood, his head —
no longer a head, slack, drooping
like a small, deflated hot air balloon. One man grasps
this ugly doll by an arm
staring at it in disbelief,
pity and fear. Others hold on
and let go, their faces
straying up and down.
A fat man in a turban
stands and stares,
satisfied with his potbelly.
Against the dark heavens
someone kneels, slowly allowing
the sheet to drop.
Everything is in darkness. The trees too.
Only the body shines.

No, not exactly. Again. From the beginning.
Soft white flesh, so it seems,
living, breathing, moving its arms,
loving even. Outside the frame,
one guesses they will put him to rest in the ground.
Put him to rest? Will he rest? Eternal rest.
No. Not exactly.

הַדְּמוּת דְּמוּת, אֲבָל
רַק לִכְאוֹרָה. הַמַּחֲזֶה יָדוּעַ,
לִכְאוֹרָה. הַדְּמֻיּוֹת,
הָעֵץ הַדָּמוּם, הָרָקִיעַ
צְבָעִים. הַצְּבָעִים צְבָעִים –
אֲבָל מִנַּיִן וּלְאָן? אֲפֵלָה. הַתְּמוּנָה
תְּלוּיָה בְּמִינְכֶן. רָאִיתִי.
רָאִיתִי? הֲלֹא
הִיא מֵאֲחוֹרֶיהָ, הִיא מִלְּפָנֶיהָ,
הִיא מִתַּחַת הִיא מֵעַל לְבַדָּהּ
כַּצִּפּוֹר הַפּוֹרַחַת
בְּהֶבֶל פֶּה אַחֲרוֹן, מְרַחֶפֶת רֶגַע
מֵעַל פָּנִים שֶׁהָיוּ
מֻכָּרוֹת, וְלֹא עוֹד, מִדַּמֶּה
לַנְּשָׁמָה –

The figure is a figure, but
only apparently. The scene is well-known,
apparently. The characters,
the bloodied, silent wood, sky,
colors — colors are colors —
but from where and where to? Darkness. The painting
hangs in Munich. I saw it.
Did I see it? Isn't it
behind, in front,
under and above, alone
like a bird flying
with its last breath, floating a moment
above a face that was
familiar and no longer resembles
a soul —

מלאך חדש

פָּנַי בְּעָרְפִּי. לְנֶגֶד עֵינַי
עִיֵּי חֳרָבוֹת, עִיֵּי חֳרָבוֹת.
תִּקְווֹת זְעוּמוֹת נִתְעוֹפְפוּ, חֲרוּכוֹת
צָנְחוּ אֶל הָאֹפֶל.
נִפְלַטְתִּי.
עָלִיתִי.
נוֹלַדְתִּי שֵׁנִית
שָׁקוּף כֶּעָשָׁן.

הַזְּמַן הָאִלֵּם
נוֹשֵׁב מִגַּן אִילָנוֹת הַיַּלְדוּת,
דּוֹחֵק בְּלִבִּי הָעִקֵּשׁ,
פּוֹשֵׁק אֶת כְּנָפַי.
אֲנִי נִדְחָף אָחוֹר לַבָּאוֹת.
מָתַי יָבוֹא הַבָּא לְכַבּוֹת אֵשׁ עֵינַי?

Angelus Novus

My face is on my back. I see
heaps of ruins, heaps of ruins.
Tiny scorched hopes flew
and fell down into the darkness.
I was cast out.
I rose up.
I was born again
translucent as smoke.

Mute time
blows out of childhood's grove,
presses on my stubborn heart,
spreads my wings.
I'm pushed back toward what's approaching.
When will the one who arrives
put out the fire in my eyes?

הנפילה

אֵצֶל שַׁאגָאל מִשְּׁמֵי-שָׁמַיִם
הוּא נוֹפֵל כְּנָפָיו כְּלַהֲבוֹת כֵּהוֹת
סוֹמְרוֹת מֵעַל גַּבּוֹ לְלֹא הוֹעִיל.
הוּא כְּמוֹ עֻבָּר שָׁמוּט מֵרֶחֶם.
בְּאֵיזוֹ מְהִירוּת
הַכֹּל חוֹלֵף, הוֹפֵךְ אֲוִיר, בִּיעָף
הַנַּסִּים הַלָּלוּ, כָּל הָעֲיָרָה
שֶׁהִתְאַסְּפָה לִקְרַאת הַמַּחֲזֶה, הַפַּחַד
הוֹתִיר בַּתָּוֶךְ שֶׁטַח רֵיק,
זְרוֹעוֹת שְׁלוּחוֹת, נָשִׁים כּוֹרְעוֹת לָלֶדֶת, אֲחֵרִים
מֵתִים מִצְּחוֹק – כְּבָר עֲצוּמִים כְּמוֹ עָנָן
וּמְכַסִּים חַיָּיו שֶׁעוֹד לְהֶרֶף-עַיִן
שָׁם מֵעַל, מַזָּל מוּזָר,
תּוֹעִים בְּמָבוֹךְ נְפִילָתוֹ.

לֹא כָּכָה אֵצֶל בְּרֶכֶל. כָּאן
רַק רֶגֶל זְעִירָה עוֹד מִזְדַּקֶּרֶת מַעְלָה
בְּעוֹד שֶׁהַשְּׁנִיָּה כְּבָר שְׁטוּפָה גַּלִּים קְטַנִּים.
דַּיָּג עָסוּק בְּחַכָּתוֹ.
בְּמִפְרָשִׂים גְּדוֹלִים נוֹסַעַת אֳנִיָּה.
רוֹעֶה, גַּבּוֹ לַיָּם, מַבִּיט בְּעֵץ כִּבְפֶלֶא מִשָּׁמַיִם.
אִכָּר מַמְשִׁיךְ בַּחֲרִישׁוֹ, כִּי אֵין לְהִשְׁתַּמֵּט
מֵעַצְבּוֹנָהּ שֶׁל אֲדָמָה וּמִטְרְחַת הַיּוֹם.
אִיקָרוֹס? מִי?
הַשֶּׁמֶשׁ כְּבָר נוֹטָה. הַחֲשֵׁכָה קְרוֹבָה.

40

The Fall

For Chagall, he falls
from the heavens, his wings dark flames
crossing uselessly behind his back.
He is like a fetus detached from the womb.
How quickly
everything passes, turns into air in startled flight,
these miniatures, the whole town
gathered to watch the scene, fear leaves
a clearing in the middle,
arms outstretched, women crouching to give birth, others
dying of laughter — so many, like a cloud
that closes in on his life in the blink of an eye there
above, strange luck,
they stray into the labyrinth of his fall.

It's not like this with Breughel. Here
only a tiny leg sticks out
while the other is washed by small waves.
A fisherman is busy with his rod.
A boat with large sails goes out to sea.
A shepherd, his back to the water, looks at a tree as though it were
          a miracle.
A peasant continues to plough, because there's no ignoring
the earth's pain and daily toil.
Icarus? Who?
The sun is already about to fall. Darkness is near.

סוס ורוכבו

רָכוּב עַל גַּב סוּס.
בִּשְׁנוֹת הַשְּׁמוֹנִים שֶׁל הַמֵּאָה הָעֶשְׂרִים
מָה עוֹשֶׂה אוֹתוֹ אִישׁ רָכוּב עַל גַּב סוּס?
הוּא אִטִּי.
הוּא אִטִּי מְאֹד.
אֵין טַעַם לַחֲזֹר.
עֲתוֹתָיו בְּיָדָיו כְּמוֹשְׁכוֹת שְׁמוּטוֹת.
אַחֲרָיו חוֹמוֹת. לְפָנָיו חוֹמוֹת.
גְּדֵרוֹת מְחֻדָּדוֹת וַחֲנִיתוֹת עֲזוּבוֹת פֹּה וָשָׁם.
הַשָּׁמַיִם אֲפֵלִים לִבְלֹעַ.
אוֹר הָאָרֶץ חִוֵּר כַּמָּוֶת.
וַאֲנִי אֵינֶנִּי
אֶלָּא מְדַבֵּר.
מֵאַיִן רוֹכֵב הָאִישׁ עַל גַּב סוּס?
לְאָן רוֹכֵב הָאִישׁ עַל גַּב סוּס?
אֵין טַעַם לְהַמְצִיא תַּחְבִּיר חָדָשׁ.
סוּס וְרוֹכְבוֹ, בֵּין כֹּה וָכֹה.
הוּא לֹא הִתְקַדֵּם גַּם לֹא פְּסִיעָה אַחַת.
גַּם לֹא מִכָּאן עַד כָּאן.
אֵין טַעַם לַחֲזֹר בָּאוֹר הַזֶּה.
הוּא מַבִּיט נִכְחוֹ.

Horse and Rider

Riding on the back of a horse.
What is that man doing riding on the back of a horse
in the 1980s?
He is slow.
He is very slow.
No point going back.
His seasons in his hands like loose reins.
Walls behind him. In front of him, walls.
Here and there sharp-edged fences and abandoned lances.
The sky darkening to swallow.
The light of the earth pale as death.
And I am not,
I merely speak.
Where does the man riding on the back of the horse come from?
Where does the man riding on the back of the horse go?
There's no point inventing a new syntax.
Horse and rider, either way.
He hasn't advanced, not even one step.
Not even from here to here.
No point going back in this light.
He sees things as they are.

שלושה רישומים סיניים

ראשון

פָּרוּם הִתְבַּלָּה בֵּין עָבִים הַסַּהַר.
סַהַר סַהַר הַנוּמָה
קוֹרְאַת הַנַּעֲרָה אֲנוּסַת צֵל
וְעֵינֶיהָ מִתְבַּהֲרוֹת בַּכֶּסֶף הַדַּק.

שני

רַמָּאי, לוֹקֶה בְּחָסֵר, מַעֲמִיד פָּנִים
כְּאִלּוּ אֶתְמוֹל נוֹלַד, סַהֲרוֹן צָעִיר וְשָׁקוּף,
וְעוֹד יַעֲלֶה וְיָבוֹא מָלֵא זָהֳרוֹ, יֵצֵא מֵאָהֳלוֹ, יֵלֵךְ גֵּיא צַלְמָוֶת –
בַּלַּיְלָה הַבָּא גַּחֲלִילִית בַּת לַיְלָה
תִּהְיֶה יוֹתֵר מַמָּשׁ מִמְּךָ –
– רוֹשֵׁם הָאִישׁ הַלָּבָן בִּדְיוֹ שְׁחֹרָה
רָכוּן עַל שְׂפַת הַבְּרֵכָה, רוּחַ קַלָּה מַרְעִידָה אֶת עֵינָיו,
לְבַל יִשְׁכַּח, לְבַל יִשָּׁכַח כָּלִיל
זֶה הָאוֹר הָרָזֶה שֶׁזְּמַנּוּ קָצָר
הַמַּגִּיהַּ עַכְשָׁו אֶת יָדָיו
וְלֹא יִהְיֶה מָחָר.

שלישי

יוֹד עֲקֻמָּה, חֲלוּדָה, לֹא כְלוּם.
אִישׁ זָקֵן טוֹרֵחַ לִמְצֹא
עוֹד אוֹת, עוֹד אוֹת, עוֹד אוֹת.
פָּגוּם וְדוֹמֵם עָלָה וְיָרַד הַיָּרֵחַ.
מְלָאכָה לְבַטָּלָה. הָאֲפֵלָה בּוֹלַעַת.
הַכְּלָבִים נוֹבְחִים עַל הַזָּר לָהֶם.
הָאִישׁ הַזָּקֵן מִתְעַקֵּשׁ.

44

Three Chinese Sketches

The First

Ripped, ragged among the clouds, the moon.
Moon, moon, veil,
calls the girl, compelled by shade,
her eyes brightening in the thin silver.

The Second

A cheat, it falls short, pretends
it was born yesterday, transparent young crescent,
and it shall rise and go in all its splendor, leaving its tent,
walking through the valley of the shadow of death —
the next night a newborn firefly
will be more real than you are —
the pale man writes in black ink
bent over the edge of the pool, a breeze causes his eyes to twitch,
so that he won't forget, so that it won't be completely forgotten,
the faint light which won't last
illuminates his hands now
won't be tomorrow.

The Third

A crooked letter, rusted, no-thing.
An old man bothers to find
a letter, and another and another.
Broken and still, the moon rises and falls.
Useless labor, the darkness swallows.
Dogs bark at strangers.
The old man insists.

תמונה ודו-שיח

הַמָּאוֹר הַקָּטָן הוּא הַמָּאוֹר הַגָּדוֹל.
הָאֲוִיר רְאִי שֶׁל מַיִם מְאָרָרִים.
בְּאוֹר הָרַע, בַּשְּׁתִיקָה
מוּטֶלֶת עִיר, נָפְלָה יְרֵכָה, כְּשֶׁרֶץ מְפֻתָּל.
רֹאשָׁהּ, פָּחוּס, בְּעַיִן מְאֻבֶּנֶת
נִבָּט בְּעֵין הָאֶבֶן שֶׁל הַמַּה-שָּׁמָם-שָׁם שָׁמַיִם.

– "אֵיזֶה צְבָעִים", אָמַרְתְּ, "אֵיזֶה צְבָעִים! כַּמָּה חַיִּים!"
– "כְּמוֹ", אָמַרְתִּי חֶרֶשׁ וּמִתְּשׁוּקָה
רָעַד קוֹלִי. "כְּמוֹ חַיִּים.
צָרִיךְ לָזוּז. יַקִּירָתִי, צָרִיךְ לְאַט
לָזוּז. הוֹלְכִים וּמְכַבִּים, סוֹגְרִים,
סוֹגְרִים אוֹתָנוּ עוֹד מְעַט."

Picture and Dialogue

The lesser light is the greater light.
The air mirrors the water of bitterness.
In the bad light, in silence,
a city sprawls, its thigh fallen like a creeping thing.
Its head, flattened, a petrified eye
reflected in the stone eye of what's-its-name, heaven.

— "What colors," you said, "What colors! So lively!"
— "Like," I said softly, my voice trembling
with passion. "Lifelike.
We've got to go. Slowly, my dear,
we've got to go. Shutting down, closing,
they'll shut us down soon."

שני ציורי זן

מָקוֹר קָדוּם
לֹא נוֹדָע:
אַוַּז הַבָּר.
מַיִם.
אֵין עֲקֵבוֹת.

אֲגַם לָבָן
תַּחַת יָדִי.

*

דַּף אַחַר דַּף אַחַר דַּף.
לִבִּי נִכְסַף
לַשֶּׁלֶג.

48

Two Zen Pictures

An ancient source,
unknown:
a wild goose.
Water.
No traces.

A white lake
under my hands.

*

Page after page after page.
My heart longs
for snow.

ארבעה חיתוכי עץ יפניים: על הזקנה

עוֹד לֹא
הִסְפִּיקוּ, כָּל
הַחַיִּים לִפְנֵיהֶם

כְּבָר לֹא.

*

בֶּן עֶשְׂרִים רוֹאֶה בְּעֵץ שֶׁהִשְׁלִיךְ אֶת עָלָיו
נֵבֶל שֶׁל עָב.
מַנְגִּינָה אַחֶרֶת
שׁוֹמֵעַ בֶּן שִׁשִּׁים.

*

מְלַטֵּף אֶת שָׁדֶיהָ הַצְּעִירִים
– סִיחַ וְעוֹד סִיחַ מִזְדַּקְּרִים בְּיָדָיו –
וְלוֹחֵשׁ כְּחוֹלֵם
תְּאוֹמֵי צְבִיָּה.

*

הַצִּפֳּרִים – כָּשׁוּף. הַכּוֹכָבִים
כְּרוּכִים אַחֲרֵי עַצְמָם.
עָזוּב. עָפָר קַר.
דָּם מְכַסֶּה דָּם.

Four Japanese Woodcuts: Old Age

They have not
yet, all
of life before them.

Won't.

*

A twenty-year-old sees a cloud harp
in the tree that shed its leaves.
A different tune
is heard by someone sixty.

*

Stroking young breasts
— colt after colt they grow erect in his hands —
he whispers as though dreaming
twin fawns.

*

The birds — enchanted. The stars
clinging to themselves.
Forsaken. Cold ash.
Blood on blood.

סלעי גיר בריגן

אַל תַּבִּיט אֶל אֲחוֹרֶיךָ.
עַיִן רָעָה מְאַבֶּנֶת.
אַל תָּמוּשׁ מִמְּקוֹמֶךָ.

אָדוֹן אֲשֶׁר שָׁמַט מַקֵּל וְכוֹבַע
זוֹחֵל עַל גְּחוֹנוֹ אֶל עֵבֶר פִּי תְּהוֹם. אֲהוּבָתוֹ
פְּרוּשָׂה, צְנוּעָה כִּפְרִי אָדָם נָשַׁר מֵעֵץ, אוֹחֶזֶת
זְהִירָה, בְּעַנְפֵי שִׂיחַ
וּמַצְבִּיעָה לְמַטָּה, אֶל הָעֹמֶק.

הַיָּם! הַיָּם!
יַכֶּה בְּמֵיתָרָיו –
שְׁתֵּי הַסִּירוֹת הַזְּעִירוֹת הַבְּהֹב לָבָן.
שְׁחָפִים – קְרִיעוֹת חֲדוּדוֹת בָּאֲוִיר –
הָיוּ וְאֵינָם.
הַחוֹף נִשְׁחַק.
סְלָעִים שֶׁל גִּיר. חַיִּים אֵין סוֹף שְׁכוּחִים עַד דַּק.
הָאוֹר שׁוֹמֵם.

גַּבְּךָ הוֹלֵךְ וּמִתְחַדֵּד, קוֹפֵא.
אֲנִי רוֹאֶה אוֹתְךָ
מְלֵא הִרְהוּרִים, מַלְבִּין
כְּמוֹ שׁוּנִית דּוֹמֵם.

Chalk Cliffs on Ruegen

Don't look back.
The evil eye petrifies.
Don't move from this spot.

A gentleman who dropped his cane and hat
crawls on his belly toward the mouth of the abyss. His lover
reclines, modest as a red fruit fallen from a tree, cautious,
holding onto the bush
pointing down, toward the depths.

The sea! The sea!
Will beat its strings —
the two small boats, a white flicker.
Seagulls — a keen cry tears the air —
were and are no more.
The shore is eroded.
Chalk cliffs. Endless life forgotten unto dust.
Desolate light.

Your back comes into focus, freezes.
I see you
filled with contemplation, whiten
like an inanimate reef.

הספינה

אוֹר מִתְעַרְעֵר וְצִנָּה חוֹדֶרֶת מֵהַקְצָווֹת
עַל מַה שֶּׁשָּׁב וְעוֹלֶה לְאַטּוֹ מִמְּצוּלוֹת כְּמוֹ
סְפִינָה בְּקוּעָה עוֹלָה וְצָפָה
מִפְרָשֶׂיהָ מְזֻקְרִים חֲדוּדִים
חוֹרְתִים בָּאֲוִיר הַזְּכוּכִית.

הָאֲנָשִׁים עַל הַסִּפּוּן, צְלָלִים רָזִים, אֵינָם שׁוֹעִים.
אוֹר מִתְחַלְחֵל. כִּמְעַט אֵין לְהַבְדִּיל
בֵּין הַדְּבָרִים וּבֵין הַלֹּא-דְּבָרִים.
הַיָּד שֶׁבָּהּ אֲנִי אוֹחֵז בַּמַּיִם לְבָנָה כְּדַג הָפוּךְ.
הַגַּלִּים, אֲפֵלָה עוֹלָה, כְּתָמִים כְּתָמִים.

The Ship

Waning light, a chill from the sides penetrates
something rising slowly from the deep like
a floating ship split in two
its pointed sails erect
etching the air like glass.

The people on board ship, thin shadows, don't notice.
Light shivers. Almost impossible to distinguish
between things and no-things.
The hand with which I grasp water is white like a fish upside down.
The waves, rising darkness, the stains, the stains.

למה

גֻּלְגֹּלֶת הַבְּדֹלַח צְלוּלָה מְאֹד.
מְלֶאכֶת מַחֲשֶׁבֶת לְעֵלָּא וּלְעֵלָּא.
תַּרְבּוּת מָיָה, כְּמִדְמֶּה.

הָאוֹר נוֹגֵעַ בָּהּ וְנִבְלָע.

עֶצֶם בִּדְמוּת דִּמְעָה
צָרָה צוּרָה לַדְּמָמָה.

אֵינָהּ מְשִׁיבָה. אֵינָהּ שׁוֹאֶלֶת.

לָמָה אַתָּה נִגְרָר לִרְאוֹתָהּ
כְּסַהֲרוּרִי
הֲלוּם חֲלוֹמָהּ?

מֵאֲרֻבּוֹת עֵינֶיהָ נִבָּט שָׁחוֹר.
אֵיזוֹ אֲפֵלָה שֶׁאֲפִלּוּ אֲפֵלָה
אֵינֶנּוּ שָׁמָּה.

Why

The skull is crystal clear.
A superb work of art.
Mayan, if I'm not mistaken.

The light touches it and vanishes inside.

Bone in the shape of a tear
gives shape to silence.

Doesn't answer. Doesn't ask.

Dazed,
why are you drawn toward it,
dreamstruck?

The eye sockets reflect black.
A darkness so dark, it's not called
darkness.

עִם שָׁבִיס כָּחֹל

לֹא קְרָאתִיהָ, הִיא בָּאָה
מִן הַלַּיְלָה הִיא בָּאָה אֵלַי
אַיָּלָה אֵין קוֹל עֵינֶיהָ
כְּשַׁלְהֶבֶת בְּגַחֶלֶת עֵינַי

שָׁבִיס כָּחֹל וְצָהֹב לָהּ
שְׂפָתֶיהָ הֵן וְלָאו
בַּת לַיְלָה, הָאוֹר הַנָּגוּעַ
עוֹטֵךְ כְּשִׂמְלָה, אֲחוֹת שָׁוְא

כְּעָנָן בְּרוּחַ פָּנַיִךְ
מִתְפָּרְמִים בְּדָמִי
שֶׁמֶשׁ שְׁחֹרָה עֵינַיִךְ
יוֹמִי אֵינֶנּוּ יוֹמִי

58

With a Blue Headband

I didn't call her, she came
out of the night she came to me
voiceless gazelle her eyes
like a flame in the embers of my eyes

she wears a blue and yellow headband
her lips yes and no
daughter of night, the stricken light
wraps you like a dress, false sister

your face, a cloud in the wind
unraveling in silence
your eyes, black sun,
my day is not my day

צבע מים שחורים

נוֹף מְקֻטָּע, כְּמוֹ תָּפוּר קְרָעִים קְרָעִים.
בְּקוֹל לֹא קוֹל יוֹרְדִים הַמַּיִם הַשְּׁבוּרִים.
פְּנֵי אֲחוֹתִי הִבְלִיחוּ וְכָבוּ בֵּין הֶהָרִים.

הַבְּקָרִים, יוֹם אַחַר יוֹם, כְּמוֹ בּוֹרוֹת.
יְמֵי הַיַּלְדוּת עֵינֵיהֶם אֶבֶן. אַל תָּרִים.
הָאֶבֶן מְקִירָה דְּמָעוֹת שְׁחֹרוֹת.

Black Watercolors

A fragmented landscape, as if sewn from rags.
In a voice-not-a-voice the broken water recedes.
The face of my sister flickers among the hills.

Mornings, day after day, like holes.
Childhood days, their eyes stony. Don't lift.
The stone pours black tears.

הסעודה האחרונה

הַצְּבָעִים דָּהוּ.
תָּוֵי הַפָּנִים מְטֻשְׁטָשִׁים.
טֶמְפֶּרָה עַל טִיחַ!
דְּבָרִים אֲחֵרִים הֶעֱסִיקוּ אֶת הַצַּיָּר. אֲבָל
עוֹד יוֹשְׁבִים כֻּלָּם לְאוֹתוֹ שֻׁלְחָן,
עוֹד נִבְצָע הַלֶּחֶם.
עוֹד נִצֶּבֶת הַכּוֹס, עוֹד נוֹף גְּבָעוֹת כְּחַלְחַל בַּגַּב.
וְגַם כִּי לֹא יִהְיֶה
אֶלָּא כֹּתֶל סָדוּק עִם כַּמָּה כְּתָמִים,
וְגַם כִּי יְטַאטְא הַכֹּתֶל –
שִׁמְעוֹן הָיָה, יַעֲקֹב הָיָה, וְכָל הַשְּׁאָר, לְתָמִיד.
הָרוּחַ הַהוֹלֵךְ סוֹבֵב סוֹבֵב עַל פְּנֵי הַשֶּׁטַח הָרֵיק
נוֹשֵׂא צִבְעֵיהֶם כְּמוֹ אָבָק הַפְּרִיחָה,
כְּמוֹ אָבָק. גַּם כִּי בָּגַד הַבּוֹגֵד,
הַנִּבְגָּד לֹא הוּקַע, לֹא אָבַד.

62

The Last Supper

The colors are faded.
Features blur.
Tempera on plaster!
The painter was occupied by other things. But
they all still sit at the table,
and still break bread.
The cup still stands, the blue landscape of hills is still at the back.
And it won't be
anything but a cracked wall with a few stains,
also because it will be ignored —
Simon was there, Jacob was, and all the others, forever.
The rising wind goes round and round the empty space
bearing paint like pollen,
like dust. And even though the betrayer did betray,
the betrayed was not condemned, not lost.

אֲבִי

יוֹם-יוֹם הֶחֱלִיף אֶת חֲלִיפָתוֹ
חֻלְצָתוֹ, לְבָנָיו, גֻּרְבָּיו, נַעֲלָיו, אֶת הַכֹּל.
לָנוּ שָׁמַר אֱמוּנִים.
יוֹם-יוֹם אַחֲרֵי שֶׁאֲכַל צָהֳרַיִם הָיָה מְנַמְנֵם
עַל גַּבֵּי הַסַּפָּה עֶשֶׂר דַּקּוֹת בְּדִיּוּק
וְאוּלַי שְׁתֵּים-עֶשְׂרֵה. הוּא לֹא הִסְתִּיר אֶת הַחוֹר
שֶׁהֻרְמַץ מֵאַחַד הַסִּיגָרִים שֶׁלּוֹ (שִׁשָּׁה מִדֵּי יוֹם בְּיוֹמוֹ)
שׁוּב שָׂרַף בָּאָרִיג הָאַנְגְּלִי. בְּנוֹסָף עַל אֵלֶּה גַּם עָשַׁן
אַרְבָּעִים "מִצְרִיּוֹת" (מוֹנוֹפּוֹל הַטַּבָּק הָאוֹסְטְרִי)
שֶׁשָּׁלַף מִקֻּפְסָה דַּקִּיקָה בְּצֶבַע כָּתֹם.
פַּעַם לָקָה בְּהַרְעָלַת נִיקוֹטִין.
בְּסִפְרִיָּתוֹ מֵאֲחוֹרֵי זְכוּכִיּוֹת עָמַד לְצַד הַיָּנֶה יוּלִיסֵס שֶׁל גּ'וֹיְס.
הַאִם הִזְמִין אֶת הַסֵּפֶר מֵרֹאשׁ, אוֹ קִבְּלוֹ מַתָּנָה?
דַּרְכּוֹ הַיּוֹמִית לֹא הוֹבִילָה אוֹתוֹ אֶלָּא עַד מִשְׂרָדוֹ וְחָזֹר.
בְּיוֹם א' יָכֹלְתָּ לִסְמֹךְ עָלָיו כְּשֶׁצָּעַד, מַקְלוֹ בְּיָדוֹ
בְּמִכְנְסֵי נִיקֶרְבּוֹקֶר קִילוֹמֶטֶר אוֹ שְׁנַיִם עַד לַפֻּנְדָּק בַּיַּעַר
לְיָד בְּאֵר-הַבַּרְזֶל, מַה שֶׁכֻּנָּה אַחַר-כָּךְ "טִיּוּל".
יָדוֹ הִבְטִיחָה שַׁלְוָה, עֵינָיו – עָתִיד טוֹב יוֹתֵר.
לְאָמוֹן כְּמוֹ שֶׁלּוֹ לֹא זָכִיתִי מֵעוֹדִי.
הַאִם חָשַׁשׁ בְּלִבּוֹ? כְּבוֹנֶה חָפְשִׁי נֶאֱמָן
לֹא גִּלָּה אֶת סוֹדוֹ. הוּא רָקַם תָּכְנִיּוֹת
וְכִמְעַט הִגְשִׁימָן. הוּא, שֶׁנָּסַע בָּרַכֶּבֶת רַק בְּכִסְיוֹת
וְאָכַל סֶנְדְּוִיץ' בְּסַכִּין וּמַזְלֵג –
יִהְיֶה לְלוּלָן, יַנִּיק זֶבֶל-עוֹפוֹת בִּשְׁבִי צִיּוֹן!
הַמִּלְחָמָה שֶׁפָּרְצָה סִכְּלָה אֶת הַכֹּל.
הוּא עָמַד קְצָת בַּצַּד וְהִזְלִיג דְּמָעוֹתָיו פְּנִימָה
כַּאֲשֶׁר נִפְרַדְנוּ בְּתַחֲנַת הָרַכֶּבֶת וְשׁוּב לֹא נוֹתַר מִמֶּנּוּ אֶלָּא
נִפְנוּף שֶׁל יָד.

My Father

Every day he changed his suit
his shirt, underwear, socks, shoes, everything.
About us, he didn't have a change of heart.
Every day after lunch he would doze
on the sofa for exactly ten minutes
or maybe twelve. He never hid the hole
that ashes from one of his (six daily) cigars
burned in the English fabric. He also smoked
Forty Austrian cigarettes called Egyptians
that he drew out of a thin orange pack.
He had nicotine poisoning once.
Joyce's *Ulysses* stood next to Heine on the shelves behind glass.
Did he order the book, or was it a gift?
His daily route led him nowhere but the office and back.
On his Sunday walk, you could count on him, stick in hand, in knickerbockers,
a kilometer or two to the inn in the forest
near the iron well, which afterwards he called his hike.
His hand promised tranquility, his eyes — a better future.
I've never been given faith like his.
Was he worried? As a proud Freemason,
he never revealed his secret. He made plans
and almost carried them out. He, who would only ride trains while
          wearing gloves
and ate sandwiches with a knife and fork —
would become a poultry farmer, would clean their waste in Shavei Zion!
The war defeated everything.
He stood a little to the side and shed a tear to himself
when we parted at the train station and all that remains of him is
the wave of a hand.

פַּעַם אַחַת עוֹד רָאִיתִי בַּחֲלוֹם: בֻּבָּה לְבָנָה
כֻּלּוֹ עָטוּף גֶּבֶס, הֻזְדַּקֵּר בְּמָלְכָּסָן בְּמְכוֹנִית דְּחוּסָה
שֶׁבָּאָה מִכִּוּוּן הַדָּנוּבָה.
הַיּוֹם מִסְתַּכֵּל הוּא בִּי מֵהַקִּיר וְשׁוֹאֵל בְּעֵינָיו
אִם אֵדַע, בֶּאֱמֶת אֵדַע, שֶׁאֵין לְהַפְרִיד
בֵּין חַיִּים וּבֵין מָוֶת, וְכִי לָשׁוֹן לְעִתִּים אֵינֶנָּה
אֶלָּא אֲבֵלוּת עַל עֵדְנָה שֶׁאָבְדָה.

I saw him once more in a dream: a white doll
all wrapped in plaster, straight-backed on a slant in a crowded car
coming from the direction of the Danube.
Now he looks at me from the wall and his eyes question
if I'll ever know, really know, one can't
separate life from death, and sometimes language is nothing but
mourning for lost tenderness.

הבית

גְּרֶסְלִינְג 57
עוֹמֵד לִמְכִירָה
הָיָה
רֶגַע שֶׁל רֶגַע
הָיָה
קֵן מָלֵא חֲלוֹמוֹת
כַּף הַמַּנְעוּל גְּבוֹהָה מִדַּי לְיַד הַיֶּלֶד
הַגִּנָּה הָאֲחוֹרִית אֲפֵרָה מִדַּי לִשְׁנֵי וְרָדִים
הַחוֹמוֹת עֲבִירוֹת מִדַּי לְרַגְלֵי הָרוֹצְחִים
וְאַף-עַל-פִּי-כֵן
הָיָה
בַּיִת לְכַמָּה שָׁנִים
אָלֶף-בֵּית לָאָחוֹת
קוֹנְכִית לְקַנַּת-נְעוּרִים
אֱמוּנַת הָאֵם

אוֹר-בֵּין-עַרְבַּיִם
חַלּוֹן שֶׁל פַּחַד
הַהוֹרִים אֵינָם שָׁבִים
הָאָחוֹת בְּשׁוּמָקוֹם

לֶךְ לְךָ מֵאַרְצְךָ וּמִמּוֹלַדְתְּךָ
וּמִבֵּית אָבִיךָ, מֵחֲלוֹם-חִנָּם.

68

Home

57 Gressling Street
is up for sale
it was
a moment of stillness
it was
a nest filled with dreams
the lock on the door too high for a child's hand
the back garden too ashen for a pair of roses
the walls too easily crossed by murderers' legs
although
it was
a home for a few years
an alphabet for a sister
a shell for the lament of youth
mother's faith
evening light
window of fear
parents don't return
sister is nowhere

go forth from your native land
and from your father's home, a baseless dream.

תצלום אחותי בכיתה היהודית הרב-גילית
בששטין, אפריל 1942

אוֹשְׁוִיץ, טְרֶבְּלִינְקָה, סוֹבִּיבּוֹר, מַיְדָנֶק, מָאוּטְהָאוּזֶן
וְכָל הַשְׁאָר –
קְלִפּוֹת מִתְפּוֹרְרוֹת עַד דַּק
עָפָר נִזְרֶה בָּרוּחַ.

רוֹצִים לִחְיוֹת.
אַתָּה רוֹצֶה.
אֲנִי רוֹצֶה.
מִי לֹא רוֹצֶה?

אֲחוֹתִי הַקְּטַנָּה
אֲחוֹתִי בַּת הַשָּׁלֹשׁ-עֶשְׂרֵה לָעַד
גּוּפֵךְ הַצִּפֳּרִי
וּפָנַיִךְ הַנְּטוּשׁוֹת-תִּקְוָה
פְּנֵי צַעַר פְּנִימָה, פְּנֵי אַלְמוּת, פָּנַיִךְ
הַכְּמוּסוֹת מִבַּעַד לְפָנַי
בְּשִׁבְתִּי בְּבֵיתִי וּבְלֶכְתִּי בַּדֶּרֶךְ וּבְשָׁכְבִּי וּבְקוּמִי
יֵאָסְפוּ אֶל הַבְּלִימָה
עִם הֵאָסְפִי אֶל הַבְּלִימָה.

ב-12 ביוני 1942 רשומה אחותי עם הורי במשלוח לאושוויץ

70

A Photo of My Sister in the Jewish Mixed-age Classroom, Šaštin, April 1942

Auschwitz, Treblinka, Sobibor, Majdanek, Mauthausen
and all the rest —
parings crumble into
finest dust sown by the wind.

One wants to live.
You want.
I want.
Who doesn't?

My little sister
my little sister, forever thirteen years old
your birdlike body
and hopeless face
a face of inner sorrow, mute, your face
hidden behind mine
when I stay at home, when I am away, when I lie down and when I get up
gathered toward nothingness
while I am gathered unto nothingness.

On June 12, 1942, my sister, along with my parents, was transported to Auschwitz.

[אָבִי הוּמַת.]

אָבִי הוּמַת.

אִמִּי הוּמְתָה.

אֲחוֹתִי הוּמְתָה.

סָבִי הוּמַת.

סָבָתִי הוּמְתָה.

שְׁאֵרֵי בְּשָׂרִי הוּמְתוּ.

חֲבֵרִים הוּמְתוּ.

נוֹבֵחַ כֶּלֶב. יֶלֶד בּוֹכֶה. רוּחַ נִלְכְּדָה בָּעֲלָוָה.

דּוֹדִי נִצַּל.

דּוֹדָתִי נִצְּלָה.

עָדָה נֶהֶרְגָה.

לוּדְוִיג מֵת.

לֵאָה מֵתָה.

דּוֹדִי מֵת.

יַעֲנְקֶלֶה מֵת.

מוֹרֶן נֶעְדָּר

שְׁמוֹנֶה עֶשְׂרֵה שָׁנִים.

שְׁמוֹנֶה עֶשְׂרֵה שָׁנִים

נֶעְדָּר מוֹרֶן.

לֹא לַחְשֹׁב! לֹא לַחְשֹׁב!

דָּן מֵת.

אֵילוּ צְעָקוֹת שָׁם בַּחוּץ. מְכוֹנִית מִשְׁטָרָה מְיַלֶּלֶת.

דּוֹדָתִי מֵתָה.

וְרְנֶר מֵת.

אַיָּה מֵתָה.

שְׁמָמִית עַל רֶשֶׁת הַחַלּוֹן.

אַוָּה מֵתָה.

נָתָן מֵת.

אֶרְנֶסְט מֵת.

עוֹזֵר מֵת.

[My father murdered.]

My father murdered.
My mother murdered.
My sister murdered.
My grandfather murdered.
My grandmother murdered.
The rest of my flesh and blood murdered.
Friends murdered.
A dog barks. A child cries. The wind is trapped in the leaves.
My uncle saved.
My aunt saved.
Ada killed.
Ludwig died.
Lea died.
My uncle died.
Yankele died.
Moran has been missing
eighteen years.
Eighteen years
Moran has been missing.
Don't stop to think!
Dan died.
Such cries outdoors. A police car wails.
My aunt died.
Werner died.
Aya died.
There's a gecko on the window screen.
Ava died.
Natan died.
Ernest died.
Ozer died.

שָׁכַחְתִּי מִישֶׁהוּ?
בִּלְבַּלְתִּי אֶת הַסֵּדֶר?
אֲנִי הוֹלֵךְ לְמַרְאָה
מַבִּיט:
אֲנִי עוֹצֵם עֵינַיִם.
אֲנִי פּוֹקֵחַ עֵינַיִם.
מַה לֹּא נָכוֹן?

Have I forgotten anyone?
Confused the order?
I go to the mirror,
look:
I close my eyes.
I open my eyes.
Is this not so?

הַיָּמִים הַגְּדוֹלִים שֶׁל הַמֵּאָה

קָנִים נוֹגְחִים אֶת הָאֲוִיר וּנְסוֹגִים, נוֹגְחִים וּנְסוֹגִים כְּמוֹ חוֹלֵי רוּחַ.
הַשָּׁמַיִם מְלֵאִים לֶהָבוֹת צְפָרִים.
הַבָּתִּים מִתְקַפְּלִים בְּלִי קוֹל, צִיתָנִים.
הָעֵצִים שָׁכְחוּ שֶׁהָיוּ פַּעַם עֵצִים.
הַבְּקָתוֹת מִתְגַּלְגְּלוֹת בָּאֵשׁ.
סוּס עוֹמֵד וְלֹא יוֹדֵעַ לְאָן.
אַחַר-כָּךְ אֵינֶנּוּ עוֹמֵד.
עַל מַדְרֵגוֹת מְיֻתָּרוֹת, חֲסֵרוֹת-יֵשַׁע
שׁוֹכֶבֶת יַלְדָּה כְּמוֹ בֻּבָּה נְפוּחָה.
גַּם אִם תּוֹלִים בָּהּ עֵינַיִם עוֹד וְעוֹד אֵינֶנָּה זָזָה.

פִּתְאוֹם מִדְבָּר.
חֶלְקֵי פָּנִים מֵאֲחוֹרֵי מִשְׁקֶפֶת.
לַמִּדְבָּר אֵין קֵץ.
מִי מִכָּל הַצְּלָלִים הַזָּעִים הַלָּלוּ
יוּכַל לִזְכֹּר אוֹתוֹ.
מִי מֵהֶם יוֹדֵעַ מַה צָּמֵא הַחוֹל.
פַּעַם אֵלֶּה וּפַעַם אֵלֶּה, בְּלָשׁוֹן יְבֵשָׁה.

מִתַּחַת לַמַּיִם עוֹלֶה צִנּוֹר
סַקְרָן כְּמוֹ עוֹרְבָּן עִם צַוָּאר שֶׁל גִּ'ירָף.
בָּאֹפֶק אֳנִיָּה כְּבָר לֹא אֳנִיָּה.
עָנָן שָׁחֹר שֶׁלֹּא יָרַד מִן הַשָּׁמַיִם עוֹלֶה מֵהַמַּיִם.
אַחַר-כָּךְ חֲשֵׁרַת עֲנָנִים.

רַגְלַיִם בּוֹסְסוֹת בַּבֹּץ.
הַבֹּץ מִתְקוֹמֵם וְנִכְנָע.

לַמֵּתִים יֵשׁ פָּנִים שֶׁלֹּא יוֹדְעוֹת כְּלוּם, שֶׁלֹּא מְגַלּוֹת כְּלוּם
שֶׁנּוּתְנוֹת לְךָ לְנַחֵשׁ אֶת הַכֹּל. רַגְלַיִם מֵעֲלֵיהֶם בִּתְנוּעָה.
רַגְלַיִם לְצַדָּם בְּלִי תְּנוּעָה. הַקְּפוּאִים נִרְאִים כְּמוֹ

76

The Great Days of the Century

The cannons gore the air and withdraw, gore and withdraw like sick spirits.
The sky is filled with flaming birds.
The houses, obedient, fold up without a sound.
The trees have forgotten they were once trees.
The huts seethe in the flames.
A horse stands, doesn't know where to go.
And then he doesn't stand.
On useless, helpless stairs
lies a girl like a swollen doll.
Even if one keeps looking at her, she doesn't move.

Suddenly a desert.
Parts of a face behind binoculars.
The desert is endless.
Who among all these shifting shadows
can remember it.
Which of them knows how thirsty the sand is.
Sometimes these and sometimes others, with a dry tongue.

A pipe rises under the water
as curious as a jay with a giraffe's neck.
On the horizon a ship no longer a ship.
A black cloud that has not descended from the sky rises from the water.
Afterwards a group of clouds.

Feet trample the mud.
The mud rebels and surrenders.

The dead have faces that know nothing, reveal nothing
that allow you to guess everything, Above them legs are moving.
Legs to the side of them don't move. Frozen, they look like

כְּמוֹ לֹא נִבְרְאוּ בְּצֶלֶם. הַשְּׂרוּפִים
אֶפְרָם הָאֲוִיר שֶׁאָנוּ נוֹשְׁמִים
חַסְרֵי מַרְאֶה.

שְׂדוֹת שֶׁלֶג אֵינְסוֹפִיִּים. הַכֹּל אֶפֶס וָאַיִן.

פִּתְאוֹם דְּקָלִים.
מִשָּׁנָה לְשָׁנָה הַזְּמַן מִתְקַצֵּר, מִשְּׁנִיָּה לִשְׁנִיָּה.
הָאֶקְרָן מְהַבְהֵב כְּמוֹ מִבְרָקִים חֲסוּמִים.
אֲנִי אָדָם שֶׁהִזְדַּקֵּן בִּשַׁלְוָה יַחֲסִית. הַטֶּלֶפוֹן צִלְצֵל
וַאֲנִי מְשׂוֹחֵחַ בְּשַׁלְוָה עִם יָדִיד, עֵינַי רוֹאוֹת.
עֵץ הָאֱגוֹז הִתְחִיל לְלַבְלֵב.
הַזֵּיתִים זוֹרִים כֶּסֶף לָרוּחַ.
צִפּוֹר נִסְפֶּגֶת בַּתְּכֵלֶת הַשְּׁחוּטָה.
זֶה הָיָה, אֲנִי אוֹמֵר בְּלִבִּי, זֶה הָיָה כְּשֶׁהָיִיתָ צָעִיר.
הֲלֹא נֶחֱלַצְתָּ מִזֶּה. הֲרֵי אַתָּה חַי.
הֲלֹא נֶחֱלַצְתָּ מִזֶּה, אֲנִי חוֹזֵר וְאוֹמֵר, הֲרֵי אַתָּה חַי.

like they were not created in God's image. The ashes
of the burned in the air we breathe
invisible.

Endless fields of snow. Everything is nothing and nil.

Suddenly palm trees.
Time grows shorter from year to year, second to second.
The screen flashes as though from blocked lightening.
I am someone who aged with relative calm. The telephone rang
and I speak calmly with a friend, my eyes can see.
The walnut tree has begun to blossom.
The olives silver in the breeze.
A bird disappears into the slaughtered blue.
This happened, I say to myself, this happened when you were young.
For surely you were saved. After all, you're alive.
For surely you were saved, I repeat, after all, you're alive.

לא חשבתי שכך

לֹא חָשַׁבְתִּי שֶׁכָּךְ זֶה יִהְיֶה
שֶׁנַּגִּיעַ לְמַה שֶּׁהִגַּעְנוּ. שֶׁבְּלִי מֵשִׂים
יֵרֵד לַיְלָה וְיִתְמַלֵּא עֶצֶב לָבָן. הִזְדַּקַּנּוּ
וְאַף-עַל-פִּי-כֵן לֹא נִרְגַּעְנוּ. וַי לִי
וַוי לָךְ שֶׁכָּךְ. שֶׁהִגַּעְנוּ לְכָאן. בְּאֶמְצַע הַחֹרֶף אָבִיב.
זֶה מַכְאִיב. חָסֵר לִי הַגּוּף שֶׁיּוֹדֵעַ לִפְרֹשׂ כְּנָפַיִם
בְּלִי מַחֲשָׁבוֹת סֵתֶר, בְּלִי סְפֵקוֹת, וּלְהִתְרוֹמֵם. שׁוּב הַקִּינוֹת הַקְּטַנּוֹת
מְעוֹפְפוֹת סָבִיב. הֲלֹא לֹא לָזֶה הִתְכַּוַּנּוּ. בִּקַּשְׁנוּ מָעוֹף, וְלוּ נָמוּךְ
וְלוּ בְּגֹבַהּ דֶּשֶׁא, אֲבָל מָעוֹף.
מְעוֹף שׁוֹבְכִים.
כִּי דָבָר לֹא יִשְׁתַּנֶּה עוֹד וְהִגַּעְנוּ לְאָן
שֶׁהִגַּעְנוּ. כִּי אֵין לָנוּ לְאָן. כִּי אֲנַחְנוּ כָּאן כְּמוֹת
שֶׁאֲנַחְנוּ. נוֹשְׁמִים בִּכְבֵדוּת. שׁוֹכְבִים זֶה בְּצַד זֶה
עַל הַפָּנִים. כִּי כּוֹכְבֵי שָׁמַיִם רְחוֹקִים.

I Didn't Expect

I didn't expect it to be this way
that we would come to this. That without noticing
night would fall and fill with white sadness. We've grown old
and yet we haven't calmed down. Woe to me
and woe to you for this. That we've arrived here. Spring in the middle
        of winter.
It hurts. I miss the body that could spread its wings
without second thoughts, without doubts, and take off. Once again
the petty laments fly around. This isn't what we meant. We wanted to fly
even if low, the height of the grass, but to fly.
The flight of the dying.
For nothing will change and we've reached where
we are. For we haven't got whereto. For we're here such as
we are. Breathing heavily. Lying side by side
face down. For the stars are far away.

יום גשום ותצלום

רַק אָמַרְתִּי: יוֹרֵד גֶּשֶׁם
וּכְבָר שׁוֹמְעִים צְלִיל אַחֵר.

אֵיזֶה מָשׁוֹשׁ, רַחַשׁ, רִשְׁרוּשׁ, לַחַשׁ חֲשָׁאִי
וּבְלִי מֵשִׂים, שְׁאָגָה שְׁלוּחַת רֶסֶן, תִּיפוּף
אֶלֶף כַּפּוֹת יָדַיִם בַּחַלּוֹן תּוֹבְעוֹת כְּנִיסָה.

עַכְשָׁו הוּא יוֹרֵד וּמְמַלְמֵל
מוֹחֵק אֶת הֶעָשָׁן, מְמוֹסֵס אֶת הָאֵפֶר
כּוֹבֵשׁ אֶת כָּל הָאֲוִיר.

אֵיזֶה דִּבּוּר לֹא דָּבוּר.
לְאָן נֶעֶלְמוּ כָּל הַשָּׁנִים, אָבַד קוֹלָן?
מְשַׁמְּשֵׁת הַחַלּוֹן הֶחָשׁוּךְ
נְבָטוֹת עֵינַיִם בְּלִי נִיעַ.

גֶּשֶׁם יוֹרֵד בְּהַשְׁקֵט, בְּהַשְׁלֵו
עַל הַקְּבָרִים הַיְשָׁנִים וְעַל הַקְּבָרִים
הָרֵיקִים. מוֹרֶה-דֶּרֶךְ חֲרִישִׁי.

לְפֶתַע נִבְעָה סֶדֶק בֵּין הֶעָבִים
סִילוֹן שֶׁל אוֹר מֵאִיר פְּנֵי יֶלֶד
עֵינָיו חַסְרוֹת יֶשַׁע מְעַט, מְעַט מִשְׁתָּאוֹת וּקְפוּאוֹת.
הַפָּנִים הַבְּהִירִים בְּהִירִים
מוּגָּנִים בָּאֵפֶר הַמַּחֲוִיר וְהוֹלֵךְ.

Rainy Day and a Photo

As soon as I say it's raining
a different sound is heard.

A certain fondling, humming, rustling, muffled whispering
and then suddenly an unrestrained roar, the patter
of a thousand hands on the window demanding to be let in.

Now it falls and mutters
erases the smoke, melts the ash
occupies all the air.

A certain talk that isn't talk.
Where did the years go, their voices?
From the dark windowpane
peer eyes that don't move.

Rain falls silently and calmly,
on old graves and on the empty
graves. A mute guide.

Suddenly there's a crack in the clouds
a jet stream of light illuminates a child's face
his eyes a little helpless, a little confused and frozen.
His pale, pale face
protected by the fading gray.

ביום הזוהר

בַּיּוֹם הַזּוֹהֵר בָּאתִי לְאָן
בָּאתִי לְכָאן בַּיּוֹם הַזּוֹהֵר?
אִישׁ הַסִּירָה הֵנִיף מָשׁוֹטוֹ וְהִפְלִיג
שׁוּב לַחוֹף הָאַחֵר. כֶּלֶב הֵרִים רֶגֶל שְׂמֹאל
שִׁירֵי קְלִפּוֹת פְּזוּרִים, הָאוֹר בְּרֹשִׁי
מְעַט. בְּלִבִּי אָמַרְתִּי. וּלְכָאן אָמַרְתִּי בְּלִבִּי בָּאתִי וְלָמָּה
בָּאתִי לְכָאן בַּיּוֹם הַזּוֹהֵר?
וְיַלְדָּה קְטַנָּה עִם צִפּוֹר בְּיָדָהּ עוֹד סְבוּרָה כִּי תּוּכַל
לַחְמֹק. גַּם יְלָדִים —
וְהֵנִיף מָשׁוֹטוֹ וְהִפְלִיג שׁוּב לַחוֹף הָאַחֵר —
בָּאִים לְכָאן. וּכְצֵל אֲנִי כָּאן בְּלִבִּי. כְּצֵל לִבִּי. לָמָּה
בָּאתִי לְכָאן בַּיּוֹם הַזּוֹהֵר?

The Shining Day

On the shining day where did I go
Is it here that I came on the shining day?
The boatman raised his pole and sailed
back to the other shore. A dog lifted a left foot,
remains of peels were scattered around, the light a little
like a cypress. I said to myself. And here I said to myself I came and why
have I come here on the shining day?
A little girl with a bird in her hand still thinks she can
get away. Children too —
and he raised his pole and sailed again to the other shore —
come here. And like a shadow I am here in my heart. Like a shadow
        my heart. Why
have I come here on the shining day?

אור אורפאי

יֵשׁ חַיִּים עִם יָד אַחַת, רֶגֶל אַחַת, רֵאָה אַחַת
כְּלָיָה אַחַת, בְּלִי רַגְלַיִם, בְּלִי יָדַיִם, עַיִן אַחַת, בְּלִי עֵינַיִם.
אֲנִי חַי עִם לֵב אֶחָד.
לֹא רָצִיתִי לְגַלּוֹת. אֵינִי יוֹדֵעַ מַדּוּעַ גִּלִּיתִי.
עַכְשָׁו יָבוֹאוּ בְּאֶצְבָּעוֹת דַּקּוֹת מְחֻדָּדוֹת
יְחַטְטוּ, יְמַשְׁשׁוּ, יִגְזְרוּ: שֶׁקֶר וְכָזָב –
אֲנִי מַסְכִּים, אֲנִי מַסְכִּים. אֲנִי
אוֹכֵל, יָשֵׁן, עוֹבֵד, שׁוֹמֵעַ מוּזִיקָה.
"מִמַּחֲשָׁבָה הַזַּכָּה שֶׁעוֹלָה לִפְנֵי הַקָּבָּ"ה
נִבְרָא בּוֹ מַלְאָךְ. וּבְמַחֲשָׁבָה שֶׁל פֻּרְעָנוּת
נִבְרָא בּוֹ שֵׁד."
אֵיזֶה פְּטָפוּט. אֵיזֶה פְּטָפוּט נוֹרָא.

כְּשֶׁטָּסִים מֵעַל עַנְנֵי קוּמוּלוּס אַפְרוּרִיִּים, אוֹר מְאֻחָר, מִתְעַמְעֵם, מְדַמִּים
מַה קַּל לָלֶכֶת, צַעַד רַךְ נִטְמָע לֹא-נִשְׁמָע שׁוּם מַאֲמָץ
לִשְׁכַּב מִבְּלִי לָקוּם עוֹד, גּוּף קַל, מְרַחֵף, כִּמְעַט לֹא גּוּף –
נוֹף מָוֶת רַךְ, תְּהוֹמוֹת מָוֶת, שֶׁמֶשׁ מָוֶת שׁוֹקַעַת, הָרֵי שְׁאוֹל עֲשׂוּיִים
פְּלוּמָה – דְּמוּיִים, דְּמוּיִים. אֵינֶנִּי חָתוּל. אֵין לִי תִּשְׁעָה חַיִּים.
לְשֵׁם מָה, לְשֵׁם מַה כָּל זֶה?
אֵינִי יוֹדֵעַ. הָאֱמֶת –
אֵיזֶה פְּטָפוּט נוֹרָא.

Orphic Light

You can live with one arm, one leg, one lung
one kidney, no legs, no arms, one eye, no eyes.
I live with one heart.
I didn't want to say it. I don't know why I did.
Now they'll come with thin, pointed fingers
to poke, probe, decree: a total lie —
I know, I know. I
eat, sleep, work, listen to music.
"From the pure thoughts that arose before The-Holy-One-Blessed-Be-His-Name
he created angels. And from thoughts of disaster
he created demons."
What nonsense. What terrible nonsense.

When flying over gray cumulus clouds, in dim, late light, one imagines
how easy it would be to go, a light step swallowed, unheard, effortless,
to lie down and never rise again, light weight, floating, almost bodiless —
a soft landscape of death, the depths of death, the death-sun sinking, the hills
          of the underworld
are made of down — images, images. I'm not a cat. I haven't got nine lives.
For what, what's all this for?
I don't know. The truth is —
what terrible nonsense.

תצלום

עֵינַיִם בְּגוֹן הַשָּׁמַיִם בַּחֹרֶף.
אֵפֶר. עָנָן. נְיָר.
עֵינַיִם בְּצֶבַע נְיָר אֵפֶר.
מְקֻמָּט קִמְעָה, נִקְרָע בְּקַלּוּת, חִיּוּךְ

רָפֶה. לֹא בָּעֵינַיִם. שְׁנֵי קַוִּים
יוֹתֵר כֵּהִים, לְמַטָּה
בַּקְצָווֹת קְצָת מִתְרוֹמְמִים.
זָוִית מְשֻׁנָּה, פֶּה

מְחַיֵּךְ, נָצוּר, לֹא פוֹצֶה, לֹא הֶגֶה, לֹא כְלוּם.
לֹא הֶבֶל, לֹא כְלוּם. פִּי נְיָר מְחַיֵּךְ.

הַפָּנִים
פְּנֵי נַעַר. אִם לְדַיֵּק, מִי
שֶׁהָיָה נַעַר, שֶׁהָיוּ לוֹ
פָּנִים.

פְּנֵי נַעַר אֶפְרִים, פְּנֵי נְיָר
מוּטָלִים עַל שֻׁלְחָן מַבְרִיק.
בִּמְהֵרָה יַצְהִיבוּ,
אֵי שָׁם, בָּעֲרֵמָה.

88

Photo

Eyes the color of the sky
in winter. Gray. Paper
cloud. Eyes the color of
gray paper. Slightly wrinkled, easily torn, a weak

smile. Not in the eyes, two lines,
darker, below,
turned up a bit at the edges.
At a strange angle, a half

smile, shut, not opening, not uttering, nothing
No nonsense, nothing. A paper mouth smiles.

A face
a boy's face. To be exact, someone
who once was a boy who had
a face.

The gray face of a boy,
the open paper face spread over a shiny table.
It will yellow quickly,
somewhere, in a pile.

אלה תולדות

בְּמְחִי יָד אַחַת
יִמָּחֲקוּ אוֹתָנוּ
כְּמוֹ מִשְׁוָאָה שְׁגוּיָה מֵעַל הַלּוּחַ
כְּמוֹ זְבוּב טוֹרְדָנִי.
אֶת הַגּוּף יְמוֹסְסוּ עַד יָמוֹג, יִתְנַדֵּף כָּלִיל
לֹא יַשְׁאִיר אַחֲרָיו אֶלָּא אֲוִיר מַצְחִין
כְּאִלּוּ מֵעוֹלָם
לֹא הָיִינוּ.

מֵהַבַּיִת הַזֶּה גַּם זֵכֶר
סִימָנֵי הַקִּירוֹת בַּקַּרְקַע
לֹא יִהְיֶה אֶפְשָׁר לְזַהוֹת.
מַה שֶּׁהָיָה הָיָה.
הָיָה?
אֵין לָדַעַת.

וְהַמָּקוֹם כֻּלּוֹ
לֹא יֵהָפֵךְ, לֹא יִבָּקַק
לֹא יֵהָרֵס, לֹא יִנָּתֵץ –
הוּא יִבָּלַע בְּתוֹךְ עַצְמוֹ
יֶהֱמֶה מְרֵיקוּת.
– כְּבָר עַכְשָׁו לֹא גְּעִיָּה
לֹא צְנִיפָה, לֹא פְּעִיָּה
אֲפִלוּ לֹא דִּבּוּר.
הוּא יִטָּמַע בְּקוֹץ וְחָרוּל
שָׁמִיר וָשַׁיִת.

History

With the swoop of a hand
we will be erased
like a mistaken equation from the blackboard,
like an annoying fly.
The body will melt until it vanishes, evaporates
completely, only fetid air left behind
as if we never
were.

Of this house not even a trace
of walls on the ground
will remain.
What was is gone.
Was?
No way to know.

And this whole place
will not be turned upside down, wasted
ruined, shattered —
but will swallow itself,
roar vacantly.
— There is no lowing even now,
no whinnying, no bleating,
not even talk.
It will become nettles, brambles
briars and thorns.

מִי שֶׁיָּבוֹאוּ אַחֲרֵינוּ
אִם יָבוֹאוּ אַחֲרֵינוּ
לֹא יֵדְעוּ דָּבָר
יִשְׁתַּעַשְׁעוּ, אִם יִשְׁתַּעַשְׁעוּ
וּלְשׁוֹנָם תִּהְיֶה נְקִיָּה
מִמִּלִּים כְּמוֹ "אֵלֶּה תוֹלְדוֹת".

Whoever comes after us
if anyone comes after us
will not know a thing,
will fool around, if they fool around,
their language cleansed
of words like "history."

השתנויות

אֵיךְ הַשֶּׁמֶשׁ מִזְדַּוֶּגֶת עִם עָנָן!
אֵיךְ הָרוּחַ מְשַׁנֶּה צוּרוֹת עֵצִים!
רֵיחַ גֶּשֶׁם בָּאֲוִיר!
הוֹ, כָּל הַשִּׂמְחָה הַזֹּאת!

גַּם אַחֲרֵי.

Changes

How the sun couples with the cloud!
How the wind changes the shape of trees!
The scent of rain in the air!
Oh, all this joy!

After me as well.

Notes

"Postcard to my Soul Mate": "Paris des rêves," the poem translates for us, is "Paris of dreams." In this case it also denotes the title of a 1950 album by the Lithuanian-Jewish photographer Izis (Israëlis Bidermanas) who joined the French Resistance and survived the Holocaust, and whom Ruebner later met. The photographs are accompanied by texts by writers and poets.

"Postcard from Vienna": In the original Hebrew poem, "A victim doesn't have to be ashamed because he was/ a victim." In the English translation, however, the poet asked us to replace the word "victim" with the word "hangman." Ruebner says that this ironic reference to the Austrian collaborators with the Nazis, who after the war called themselves "victims," would be lost on contemporary readers.

"Postcard from Šaštin: Autumn bonfires": The opening bracket preceding the words "are they walking with their suitcases" is not matched by a closing parenthesis in the original poem either; the lack of an ending is purposeful. The peculiarity of punctuation perhaps underscores the way that the speaker's memory of his family has been abruptly frozen in time. He is focused on the moment of their deportation to the death camps, a moment he can imagine because he is familiar with the place they were taken from. In a more positive light, his parents and sister are still alive here. Of course, post-traumatic suffering is always happening in the here-and-now. As a line in the poem says, "In memory there is no past tense."

"The Ambassadors": Hans Holbein, 1533, National Gallery, London.

"The Youths" and "The Smile": unidentified Greek statues and torsos.

"The Descent from the Cross": Rembrandt van Rijn, c. 1633, Bayerische Staatsgemäldesammlungen (Bavarian State Painting Collections), Munich.

"Angelus Novus": Paul Klee, 1920. Israel Museum, Jerusalem. In his notes to this poem, Ruebner cites Walter Benjamin's famous lines from his essay, "Theses on the Philosophy of History" (Benjamin, *Illuminations*, ed. Hannah Arendt, tr. Harry Zohn, NY: Schocken, 1978, 257–258):

> A Klee painting named 'Angelus Novus' shows an angel looking as though he is about to move away from something he is fixedly contemplating. His eyes are staring, his mouth is open, his wings are spread. This is how one pictures the angel of history. His face is turned toward the past. Where we perceive a chain of events, he sees one single catastrophe which keeps piling wreckage upon wreckage and hurls it in front of his feet. The angel would like to stay, awaken the dead, and make whole what has been smashed. But a storm is blowing from Paradise; it has got caught in his wings with such violence that the angel can no longer close them. The storm irresistibly propels him into the future to which his back is turned, while the pile of debris before him grows skyward. This storm is what we call progress.

Ruebner adds that "my poem rests on Benjamin's words. It is not about the angel of history, though, but about my personal angel."

"The Fall": Marc Chagall, "The Fall of Icarus," 1975, Centre Georges Pompidou, Paris; Breughel the Elder, "Landscape with the Fall of Icarus," 1555, Les Musées royaux des Beaux-Arts, Brussels.

"Horse and Rider": Simone Martini, "Guidoriccio da Fogliano," c. 1328, Palazzo Publico, Siena.

"Three Chinese Sketches": Ruebner has not identified these except to say that he saw them in Stockholm.

"Picture and Dialogue": Max Ernst; Ruebner has not identified the specific work.

"Two Zen Pictures" and "Four Japanese Woodcuts: Old Age": unidentified.

"Chalk Cliffs on Ruegen": Caspar David Friedrich, c. 1818, Oskar Reinhart Museum, Winterthur, Switzerland.

"The Ship": Joseph Turner, "Peace—Burial at Sea," 1842, Tate Gallery, London.

"Why": the work is unidentified.

"Black Watercolors": Hans Hartung, no venue stated.

"The Last Supper": Leonardo da Vinci, 1494–1498, Convent of Santa Maria delle Grazie, Milan.

"Home": The poet lived with his family at 57 Gressling Street. The citation "go forth from your native land/ and from your father's home" is from Genesis 12:1 (Jewish Publication Society).

"The Great Days of the Century": the title refers to a documentary made by French television in 1984.

Acknowledgments

On Time: *Late Beauty* (*Yofi meukhar*, 2009)
Uruguay-Ghana 2010: *Contradictory Poems* (*Shirim sotrim*, 2011)
Postcard to my Soul Mate: *Contradictory Poems*
Postcard from the Hebron Area: *Late Poems* (*Shirim meukharim*, 1999)
Postcard from Vienna: *Late Poems*
Postcard from Pressburg-Bratislava: *Late Poems*
Postcard from Šaštin: Autumn bonfires: *Late Poems*
Postcard from Zurich: *Late Poems*
Postcard from London: *Late Poems*
Postcard from Jerusalem: *Late Poems*
The Ambassadors: *Statue and Mask* (*Pesel veh-masekah*, 1982)
The Youths: *Statue and Mask*
The Smile: *Statue and Mask*
Descent from the Cross: *Statue and Mask*
Angelus Novus: *Statue and Mask*
The Fall: *Statue and Mask*
Horse and Rider: *Statue and Mask*
Three Chinese Sketches: *Statue and Mask*
Picture and Dialogue: *Statue and Mask*
Two Zen Pictures: *Statue and Mask*
Four Japanese Woodcuts: *Statue and Mask*
Chalk Cliffs on Ruegen: *Statue and Mask*
The Ship: *Statue and Mask*
Why: *Statue and Mask*
With a Blue Headband: *Statue and Mask*
Black Watercolors: *Statue and Mask*
The Last Supper: *Statue and Mask*
My Father: *Almost a Conversation* (*Keemat sikha*, 2002)
Home: *Almost a Conversation*
A Photo of my Sister: *Almost a Conversation*

[My father murdered]: *Almost a Conversation*
The Great Days of the Century: *Late Poems*
I Didn't Expect: *Late Poems*
Rainy Day and a Photo: *Almost a Conversation*
The Shining Day: *Late Poems*
Orphic Light: *Hastened to His Place (Veh-el makomo shoef,* 1990)
Photo: *No Return (Ain lehasheev,* 1971)
History: *Almost a Conversation*
Changes: *Late Poems*

Contributor Biographies

Tuvia Ruebner has published 15 volumes of poetry and several non-fiction books in Israel, and ten books in Germany. He has received every major literary prize in Israel, including the prestigious Israel Prize in 2008 and the Prime Minister's Prize (twice), and numerous prizes in Germany, including the Konrad Adenauer Literature Prize in 2012. Born in Slovakia, he immigrated to Mandatory Palestine in 1941, and eventually settled in Kibbutz Merhavia where he continues to live today. His poems have been translated into many languages, and he has translated the works of S. Y. Agnon into German, and Goethe into Hebrew. Ruebner also published a book of his photographs of Israel, Europe and Nepal. He is Professor Emeritus of Comparative Literature at the University of Haifa.

Poet and translator **Lisa Katz** earned her PhD at Hebrew University in Jerusalem. Editor of the Israeli pages of *Poetry International Rotterdam*, Katz is translator of Hannan Hever's study of 1940s Hebrew poetry *Suddenly the Sight of War*, and the poetry volumes *Approaching You in English*, by Admiel Kosman (Zephyr Press), and *Look There*, by Agi Mishol (Graywolf Press). She is the author of a poetry chapbook, *Are You With Me* (Finishing Line, 2016).

Shahar Bram is the author of several books of poetry, most recently *She'on Hatziporim* [A Birds' Clock], and two novels. Among his scholarly works are *A Memento: Poetry, Photography, Memory* (The Bialik Institute, 2017) and *Charles Olson and Alfred North Whitehead, An Essay on Poetry* (Bucknell University Press, 2004). He teaches in the Department of Hebrew and Comparative Literature at the University of Haifa.